George Müller

Joan Ripley Smith

 BOOKS

EP BOOKS
Faverdale North
Darlington
DL3 0PH, England

www.epbooks.org
sales@epbooks.org

EP BOOKS are distributed in the USA by:
JPL Fulfillment
3741 Linden Avenue Southeast,
Grand Rapids, MI 49548.

E-mail: sales@jplfulfillment.com
Tel: 877.683.6935

First published 2014

British Library Cataloguing in Publication Data available
ISBN: 978-1-78397-019-3

Contents

Timeline

1805 (27 September)	Born in Kroppenstaedt, Prussia
1825	Becomes a Christian after attending prayer meeting
1829 (March)	Travels to London to train at missionary society
1829 (summer)	In Teignmouth, meets Henry Craik and has 'second conversion' studying God's Word
1830	Becomes pastor at Ebenezer Chapel, Teignmouth, and marries Mary Groves (born *c.* 1797)
1832	George Müller and Henry Craik move to Bristol
1832 (September)	Lydia Müller born
1834	Scriptural Knowledge Institution established
1836 (April)	First orphan home opens on Wilson Street for thirty girls
1837 (June)	Queen Victoria begins reign

1849 (June)	First Orphan House opens at Ashley Down
1853 (May)	Anthony Norris Groves dies in Bristol (b. 1795)
1866 (January)	Henry Craik dies (b. 1805)
1870	Orphan House Number 5 opens (January); Mary Müller dies (February)
1871	Lydia marries James Wright (*c.* 1824–1905); Müller marries Susannah Sangar (*c.* 1820–1894)
1875	Begins preaching tours (travels for seventeen years)
1894	Susannah Müller dies
1898 (10 March)	George Müller dies at Orphan Home Number Three, aged ninety-two

Introduction

It has been well over a century since the death of George Müller (1805–1898) and, sadly, fewer and fewer of each ensuing generation have been acquainted with the remarkable story of the man who believed unreservedly in the power of prayer. In his lifetime, Müller was known worldwide for his work with orphans in Bristol, and all who were familiar with the homes on Ashley Down knew that George Müller asked no one but God to provide for the needs of the thousands of children in his care, and that God never failed to provide. His influence was far-reaching. One of the most singular stories in his biography illustrates how universally he was known for his message of the living God's readiness to answer prayer. While on a speaking tour in the United States, Mr and Mrs Müller decided to take a few extra days to see the acclaimed Yosemite Valley, a more out-of-the-way destination than either of them expected. They were transported to the valley by a long and bumpy stagecoach ride. On the return trip, after twelve hours on the primitive road, the coach slowed to pass another wagon.

It carried a man and woman who had pulled to the side of the narrow dusty track to let the larger stagecoach go by. The woman surprised everyone by standing up and asking loudly: 'Is that George Müller?'

'It is,' came the reply.

'Then I must shake hands with you, sir! I have read your *Life of Trust*, and it has been a great blessing to my soul.'

The Müllers shook hands with the woman and man through the coach window, and before any further introductions or pleasantries could occur, the stagecoach lurched on ahead, and the woman shouted out to the fast-departing wagon the best favour she could ask of the man from Bristol: 'Pray for me!'

Note

The reader may find the following information on money values useful in understanding some of the economics of nineteenth-century England in relation to events in the narrative. To place these amounts in context, a middle-class worker might receive 40 to 50 pounds per year in income. A pound in paper form was called a note, and in the form of a gold coin, a sovereign. There were twenty shillings in a pound, and twelve pence in a shilling. A farthing was one-quarter of a penny (one pence). A crown was five shillings, and a guinea was a gold coin worth twenty-one shillings.

1

An unsound start

Herr Müller fumed. *It has to be George. There's no other explanation.* Larger and larger amounts of money had been disappearing from the desk of the Prussian tax collector, and he couldn't help but think of his ten-year-old son. The year was 1815, and Herr Müller was convinced that in order to get by in those times, it was important for his boys to learn about managing money. He gave George and his brother, older by two years, a generous allowance, much larger than that of the average boy in the town of Heimersleben, Prussia (later Germany). But George never seemed to have enough — the money went through his hands like water, and when the time came to account for the expenditures, he invented stories to tell to his father.

The perturbed tax collector counted the total cash on his desk again, and summoned his son to the study. Knowing George would never admit to the theft, he planned to catch him red-handed. With George in place, he left the room, asking him to wait there momentarily. When he returned,

Herr Müller saw immediately that some coins were missing from the bait. George, who stubbornly denied that he had taken any, was no match for his father's obstinacy. He searched George from head to toe, and found the missing coins hidden in his son's shoe. Feeling the heat of his father's fury in the form of a beating, George afterwards had deep regrets — regrets that he had been caught, vowing only to be more clever the next time he schemed to deceive his father.

Despite his habitual lies and heedlessness, George was his father's favourite, a situation which was unhealthy for both brothers. Herr Müller had plans for his younger son. He knew George's intelligence would allow him to succeed in a lucrative profession once he was educated, and the ambitious father chose Lutheran pastor as the preferred occupation. The Müllers were not particularly religious or interested in spiritual things, only dutifully observing the obligations of members of the Lutheran Church, but the position of minister in the Prussian state church paid well. Herr Müller considered George's education a family investment, so when George was about eleven, he was sent with his brother to the cathedral classical school at nearby Halberstadt, where he could begin the sort of education a pastor would need.

Herr Müller continued to give his boys generous allowances at school, but George had learned nothing about using it wisely. In fact, his spending habits and general behaviour became worse and worse, the curriculum at the cathedral school seeming to have no beneficial effect on him. It was in the evenings, after his classes, when he fell into trouble. By the time he was fourteen, seldom did he spend time studying in his room, but left in the dark to meet his friends at taverns where he wasted large amounts of money on drink and card games.

Little is known of George's mother, except that on the night she suddenly became ill and died, George was out playing cards until the early hours of the morning and could not be found. The next day, Sunday, he spent more time with his fun-loving friends, imbibing at a tavern, then strolling the streets half-drunk. On Monday, he casually attended his first confirmation class — religious instruction to prepare him for communion. It was when he returned to his lodgings after the class that his father finally caught up with the errant boy. He had come to take George and his brother to Frau Müller's funeral in Heimersleben.

The death of his mother seemed to have little impression on George. It never gave him pause to think about the serious things in life, nor did his religious instruction — as he admitted in his memoirs that three or four days before his confirmation he was guilty of 'gross immorality'. In the church vestry, the day before confirmation, George made confession to the minister as was custom. It is not known whether George confessed to the immorality, but we do know that on the eve of his first sacrament, he pocketed all but one-twelfth of the fee his father had sent for the clergyman. And so George took his first communion on the Sunday after Easter, 1820, in his own words, 'without prayer, without true repentance, without faith, without knowledge of the plan of salvation...' (see Note, p.19).

Tall and slim, with a confident air and money in his pocket, George seemed to have no trouble attracting the attention of at least one young lady. While visiting his aunt and uncle in Brunswick a few weeks after confirmation, he became acquainted with a girl he identified only as a 'young female who was a Roman Catholic'. She later played at least some part in what was the most scandalous escapade of George's life.

In the summer of 1820, George's father was offered work in Schoenebeck, and so the Müller home, which had been in Heimersleben for eleven years, was uprooted. This would not be the first move for George, though he may not have remembered leaving his birthplace, Kroppenstaedt, when he was four. George had in mind to transfer to the cathedral school close to his father's new residence and, to his credit, he had good intentions. He knew his life was out of control and reasoned that a change of friends might somehow make things better. He sincerely resolved to improve, but only to make his life less troublesome, not to please God, for whom he had no regard. And so, depending on his own moral strength, George left the cathedral school in Halberstadt only to find opportunity for more serious trouble. He was allowed permission to stay at the old house in Heimersleben temporarily, his father reasoning that he might be of use there. Repairs needed to be made to the home before it could be rented out and, strangely, Herr Müller trusted to George the job of overseeing the work. He was fifteen at the time.

Idle and unsupervised, George's bad habits grew even worse. Large amounts of money passed through his hands from debts he was allowed to collect for his father, and George took full advantage, taking in money but not reporting the payments. He convinced his father to let him stay yet a few more months, now to study under Dr Nagel, a learned man who privately tutored pupils. In time, George was in possession of a good amount of money, and in the autumn of the next year, after his sixteenth birthday, he decided to fully enjoy its use.

He concocted a story for Dr Nagel, and headed north to Madeburg where he enjoyed six days of excess. Nearby was the town of Brunswick, the home of his female friend and his next destination. Staying in an expensive inn while enjoying her company, George soon found himself out of funds. Not wanting to leave the area, he situated himself at another hotel in a nearby village, where he was required to leave his best clothes as security for payment when it was detected he had no money. Hoping he could get by again at yet another establishment on the way home without paying, he walked to Wolfenbuttel. When the time came to settle the bill at the inn there, George planned to surreptitiously leave, but found the window too high for an exit, and was caught in his efforts to slip quietly out of the yard.

The innkeeper at Wolfenbuttel showed him no mercy, and George was escorted to the village jailhouse by two soldiers and a police officer. There, his high-class manners and educated way of speaking did nothing to impress the no-nonsense officials. Like any other criminal he was fed coarse bread and water, only vegetables for dinner, and was not allowed to leave the gloomy iron-barred cell. Even his request for a Bible was turned down. Lest the reader be hopeful that George finally had a change of heart and was searching for God's ways, it should be noted that he was suffering from extreme boredom and thought the Bible might at least help him to pass the time. The following events show the state of his heart.

After a few days of imprisonment, George was put in with another prisoner — a thief. Conversation in that dark cell turned to bragging of clever and daring exploits; and George, not satisfied with relating the many disreputable episodes in his life, invented others even more outrageous. After ten or twelve days, the two had a falling out. It would be difficult to say who had first grown disgusted with the other, but the result was sulky silence for days upon end, until George was finally released. Herr Müller had sent the required fine to the police — enough to pay for restitution to the innkeeper, the cost of his keep for twenty-four days in jail, and the coach fare back home to Heimersleben. There George waited with suspense for two days while his furious father travelled from Schoenebeck.

His punishment began with a severe beating. He was then taken home to Schoenebeck by Herr Müller and informed that after Easter he would be enrolled in a classical pre-university school in Halle known for its discipline and close supervision. In order to reverse this turn of events, George knew he must muster all his resources, renewing his studies with increased diligence, and even taking on students of his own, instructing them in Latin, French, arithmetic and German grammar. In addition to earning more than his keep through tutoring, he was polite, helpful and charming. Herr Müller soon forgave George of his flagrant delinquencies, as George had hoped, and agreed to let his son stay at home for a while longer, until Michaelmas (29 September). George may have fooled his father into thinking he had changed for the better, but he was still committing a great many hidden sins, being unconcerned about the One-Who Knows-All.

After Michaelmas, Herr Müller would not consent to have his son out of school any longer, and was satisfied when George told him he was travelling to Halle to be examined for entrance to the pre-university school his father had chosen. George, however, had no intention of enrolling in a school where he would have so little freedom, and travelled west to Nordhausen instead of down the road to Halle. There he presented himself for examination by the director of the 'gymnasium' in that city, convinced that the school would be more to his liking. The whole web of lies wasn't exposed until just a few days before the term began, and Herr Müller was livid. George creatively explained and pleaded, and soon he was happily on his way to Nordhausen.

Rising each morning at 4.00am to study, and earning top grades, George was held up as an example by the school director, in whose home he boarded. The two of them formed a friendship, taking companionable walks and conversing in Latin. Given that he was living in the director's home, and spent so much time studying, it seems incredible that George could get himself into trouble, but such was his ability to lead a double life. First, he became ill (later attributing the sickness to his wicked habits), and was confined to his room for thirteen weeks, nursed by the director's wife. After recovering, he further felt the effects of his indulgent choices when he fell into overwhelming debt. The allowance that was sent by his father to cover basic expenses was spent before it even arrived, and George was desperate.

He could, by this time, lie without blinking, and hatched a plan that involved deceiving his own friends. He showed his just-received allowance money to some of them, and then purposely damaged the locks on his trunk and guitar case. Rushing into the director's office with his jacket only half on, he announced in a shocked voice, 'Someone has stolen all my money!' His sympathetic friends felt so sorry for him that they raised the cash among themselves to replace the 'stolen' amount. Now he had doubled his allowance, and was granted an extension on some of his loans after pointing to his unfortunate experience.

George's conscience wasn't entirely dead. He regretted the whole episode. The director never fully trusted him after that, and George felt especially guilty around the director's wife, who had so selflessly nursed him during his long illness. At times he did try to reform himself, especially when he partook of the Lord's Supper two times a year with his fellow students. With the Bread of the Table in his mouth, George took an oath on one or two occasions to become better, hoping the solemn circumstances would make it so. His resolutions, however, never lasted more than a few days.

After two years at Nordhausen, George was looking forward to university, and he and his father were, for a change, agreed on where he should go — to the University of Halle. For generations, the graduates of its theology department had been held in high esteem and were called to well-paying positions in the larger Lutheran churches. That's exactly what George was hoping for, and his father was of the same mind.

Note

Quotations, unless otherwise specified, are from George Müller's autobiography, *A Narrative of the Some of the Lord's Dealings With George Müller*, the first volume published in 1837 and subsequent volumes added as the years went on. An American edition was published as *A Life of Trust*.

2

Regeneration

George had never like Beta. In fact, when they were students together four years before at the cathedral school in Halberstadt, he despised him. Beta was quiet and serious, always responsible, always seeming to hold himself above the type of activities of George and his friends — *that* sort of boy. And there he was, sitting in the tavern at Halle with some of the regulars.

George did the unexpected.

'Hello, Beta. It's so nice to see you again!' he said, offering his hand.

George reasoned he needed new friends. Already, after only a few months at Halle, he was deep into debt from his drinking and card playing, his constant need to be entertained at the theatre, billiard hall, or ballroom, and his compulsion to own the things a man of the world would possess. He was reduced to pawning his watch and some of his clothing. If he kept that up, and word got out, no parish would ever choose him as their minister. George thought a young man like Beta could pull him away from bad influences with a strength of character he himself didn't have.

Ironically, now that George was officially a divinity student of the Lutheran Church, he had government permission to preach in the pulpit. Preaching by the unauthorized was not allowed, even in small settings; but young George Müller, despite the confidence of the Prussian government, was by no means qualified to do any ministering. God had no part in his life, and the new divinity student showed no interest in studying the Bible. In fact, though George owned a great many books, the 'Holy Bible' was not among the titles.

George and Beta became close friends, but their relationship did George no good, at least not in the way he had hoped. Beta also had an agenda the evening they met in the tavern. He felt the pull of attraction to a lifestyle that looked so appealing to an outsider, and hoped George would introduce him into his fun-loving society.

And so George was able to pull Beta into his schemes, the boldest being a plan he impulsively concocted for the summer vacation. He had always wanted to travel to Switzerland, and the fact that he and his friends had neither passports nor money didn't deter him. George masterminded the forging of parental signatures, and encouraged three of his friends, including Beta, to pawn their books and other personal articles to fund the trip. Ever devious, he gave a plausible explanation to his father as to why he would not be home for the coming few weeks, and for over forty carefree days the boys hiked, discovering crystal-blue lakes and breathtaking mountain vistas. They travelled as far as Mount Rigi, and George, in awe, felt he had achieved the desire of his heart. Looking back however, later in life, he declared that even then he wasn't truly happy. Perhaps he experienced some guilt pangs for his thieving on the excursion to Switzerland. He had kept the purse for the others, and was all along paying much less than his share of the expenses.

The hiking trip was a turning point for Beta. Suffering terrible regret at the whole affair, the miserable young man confessed all to his father when he got home, and began to set himself on another path.

One afternoon in November 1825, a Saturday, Beta and George took a walk together under the autumn leaves at Halle. Before they parted at their return, Beta mentioned that he was attending meetings on Saturday evenings at the home of a Christian. 'And what goes on at these meetings?' George asked.

'They read the Bible,' said Beta cautiously. 'They sing and pray and then someone normally reads a sermon.' George was unaccountably delighted, wanting to go along. Beta, taken aback, was hesitant to bring him, thinking a Bible study would not be to George's liking and perhaps even worried that George wouldn't participate respectfully. George insisted, and finally Beta agreed to call for him that evening. George always remembered his visit that night to Herr Wagner's home where the Bible study was held. He made an apology for coming uninvited, but was welcomed with unexpected warmth and an offer to return at any time: 'house and heart are open to you,' Herr Wagner had said. They all sat down and started by singing a hymn, then prayed, kneeling on the floor. George had never seen anyone kneel in prayer, or, for that matter, anyone petitioning God in sincere faith, believing he was heard. The same man who led in prayer went on to read a chapter from the Bible and then a printed sermon (it was read since no one in the group was licensed to expound the Bible — other than George, that is). They closed the meeting with another hymn and a prayer, and as Herr Wagner prayed, George thought to himself, *I couldn't pray as well as this man, though I've had much more schooling.*

The evening's meeting had been much like the regular weekly gatherings that Beta attended, and so on the way home he was startled to hear George say, 'All we have seen in our trip to Switzerland and all our other pleasures are nothing in comparison with tonight.' Lying in bed that night, George felt happy and peaceful, not knowing exactly why, but in the morning he decided he couldn't wait until the next Saturday night meeting. He went back that day to Herr Wagner's to learn more about God and his Word, and the next day, and several days after that. He recorded his new discoveries:

> It had pleased God to teach me something of the meaning of that precious truth: 'God so loved the world, that He gave His only begotten Son, that whosoever believeth in Him should not perish, but have everlasting life.' I understood something of the reason why the Lord Jesus died on the cross, and suffered such agonies in the Garden of Gethsemane: even that thus, bearing the punishment due to

us, we might not have to bear it ourselves. And, therefore, apprehending in some measure the love of Jesus for my soul, I was constrained to love Him in return. What all the exhortations and precepts of my father and others could not effect; what all my own resolutions could not bring about, even to renounce a life of sin and profligacy: I was enabled to do, constrained by the love of Jesus.

The distinct change in George Müller was obvious to everyone. He gave up his former friends, no longer visited the tavern, and resolved to combat his habitual practice of telling falsehoods. And on the occasions he stumbled (there were a great many at the beginning), he sorrowfully prayed for forgiveness from God. He wanted to share the wonderful news of God's love and forgiveness with anyone who would listen, but had discouraging reactions; most of his fellow students laughed at him, and some ridiculed him for his piety. An enthusiastic letter he sent to his father and brother about his new faith was met with an angry response. Still, he was resolved to stand on the side of Christ, his determined and driven personality being put to a new and sanctified use.

In the new year of 1826, George, full of committed energy, began reading 'missionary papers', literature put out by mission boards informing the Christian community of specific works in other countries. He was captivated by the thought of sharing the truth of God with people in darkened parts of the world who, like the old George, had never heard the gospel. He soon felt God might be calling *him* to be a missionary. This was a matter of frequent prayer at that time and, as shall be seen, at recurring periods in George

Müller's life. A visiting missionary, Hermann Ball, made a deep impression on him as he was pondering the future. Well educated and from a wealthy family, Mr Ball, instead of enjoying the advantages of his position in life, chose to go to the Jewish people in Poland to sow the seeds of the gospel. *Is this the sort of work God wants me to do?* wondered George. *If so, I am willing*, he prayed, feeling a great peace in surrendering himself to God's purposes.

German missionary institutions required parental permission before a candidate could be considered, and George, now ready to take this step, scheduled a trip home to Schoenebeck. His father was not pleased that George was contemplating missions work. He pointed out that he had invested a great deal of money in his education, and had hoped his son could provide for him a comfortable retirement in a church parsonage. All this now, it seemed, would come to nothing, and Herr Müller's anger rose as George refused to give way. He exploded with: 'If you do this I will no longer consider you my son!' Then, even more difficult for George to witness, he broke into an unexpected weeping and pleading: 'George, I beg of you. Don't waste your time as a missionary.' George remained steadfast, and credited God for the grace to do so.

Upon return to Halle, he determined that he would no longer ask for or take any of his father's money for the remaining two years of university. It wouldn't be right, he reasoned, when there was no chance of fulfilling his expectation of having a clergyman with a good living in the family. This *was* a new George.

The uncertainty in George's finances set the stage for a series of seemingly random events which would play a part in his future work. The most important development was that he now had opportunity to see how God would provide for his temporal needs. George Müller leaned on two resources for help: prayer and advice from other Christians. One whose advice he particularly valued was Dr Tholuck, the new professor of theology at Halle. The kindly Christian man took an interest in George, and proposed a way for him to earn money — three professors visiting Halle from America needed someone to teach them German and to write out lectures. (One of these men was Charles Hodge of Princeton Seminary.) George was paid generously for this work, and it provided more than enough to meet his living expenses. 'Thus the Lord made up to me the little which I had relinquished for his sake,' he remarked. It addition to providing funds, the job must also have been a learning experience, because though George was able to communicate proficiently in several languages, English was not one of them.

Some may have called Professor Tholuck a pietist, though that Lutheran movement was at its peak over one hundred years before. Like the pietists, Tholuck believed that when a person became a child of God, a Christian, both his heart and his life should change — holiness of living accompanying the faith. The University of Halle had been a centre of Lutheran pietism from the seventeenth century to the middle of the eighteenth century, and there still stood a monument to the faith and hard work of the pietists in the city: a huge six-storey building complex, the August Hermann Francke orphanage. Built in 1695, the orphanage was still in operation

when George Müller arrived in Halle. A. H. Francke (1663–
1727), professor of theology in the university at that time,
began the home for children to give compassionate help
to the many waifs wandering the streets, and relied solely
on God's provision to run the institution. It was the largest
orphanage of its kind in the world, and the building itself
was the largest in Germany.

Through the ensuing years, there were always lodgings
reserved at the orphanage to house needy Halle University
theology students. George met the needy requirement,
and for a period of time had opportunity to live among the
residents of the A. H. Francke orphanage, witnessing the
busy and happy comings and goings of its two thousand
children.

George continued to pray about finding the mission field
God meant for him. Perhaps it would be the East Indies (the
'East Indies' in that time usually referred to India). Several
possibilities came to light, but then fell through. Meanwhile,
he found many opportunities near home to be used of God
in winning souls to Christ, 'though very weak and ignorant',
he admits. He passed out tracts and missionary papers by
the hundreds, continued witnessing to friends, wrote letters
to acquaintances from the past, and visited the sick, bringing
the encouragement of the gospel.

For over a year George, as a student of divinity, had been
authorized to expound the Bible, but was, in his own words,
'mercifully kept from attempting to preach...' He had felt
he didn't have enough experience in the things of God, but
when he was asked to fill in for an aged and infirmed parson,

Müller reasoned that he might be of use by memorizing another man's sermon — a godly man, of course. It took him most of a week to learn a message long enough to fill the hour, and at eight o'clock on Sunday morning he successfully recounted every word. The problem was that the lesson didn't seem to reach any farther than the front of the pulpit, his listeners showing not a flicker of understanding in their faces. It went the same way at the eleven o'clock service. There was to be another service in the afternoon, and George wanted very much to have these people hear the gospel, but didn't have a second sermon prepared. He decided to read the fifth chapter of Matthew, 'Blessed are the poor in spirit...', and commented as he went along. This plan went well, George feeling much helped as he explained in a simple way the words of Jesus, and was himself blessed by the passage. The congregation also seemed to respond, showing their understanding with great attentiveness. This was the method George Müller came to use as a matter of course in his many years of pulpit ministry.

Of great encouragement to George at that time was a Sunday night prayer meeting at the university. At first there were only about six believing students in the group, but by the time George was ready to graduate, it had grown to twenty. Dr Tholuck's reputation as a devoted and gifted Christian professor had attracted like-minded students to the school who were glad to meet together for prayer, Bible reading and singing, or a word of exhortation. In October of that year, the Sunday group had a visitor who was passing through Halle, a man whom George had already come to know two years before. It was Hermann Ball, missionary to the Jews, who sadly told the young men that because of poor health he was forced to leave his post. George, in the previous few months, had become fascinated with the Hebrew language, studying it out of pure pleasure, and now, with the thought of a critical mission field losing Mr Ball, his interest in working in the same field was aroused. However, he was at that very time waiting for correspondence regarding a position as missionary to Bucharest. And so he tried to put thoughts of Hermann Ball and the Jews out of his mind.

A few weeks later, George went to visit his friend Dr Tholuck, when out of the blue the professor asked: 'Have you ever thought about being a missionary to the Jews? I'm an agent with the London Missionary Society that does that sort of work.' Because an answer to the Bucharest work was pending, George kept his enthusiasm at bay. Ten days later it was relayed to him that because of its location in the thick of the battle between the Turks and the Russians, the missions committee decided it would not be safe to send a missionary to Bucharest. This set George to praying about a new mission field — to the Jewish people.

After prayer and advice from trusted Christian friends, George met with Dr Tholuck and offered himself to the 'London Society for Promoting Christianity Among the Jews.' At Easter in 1828, George Müller finished his university studies, and a few months later, in June, he received a letter from the London Society accepting him as a missionary student for a probationary period of six months. There was one provision: he would have to go to London for the six months. He wasn't excited about the six-month training period, but conceded that the Society should take the chance to get to know him, and he them, in order to have a good working relationship.

At that point in time George was twenty-two, but the Prussian government required even adult missionary candidates to get parental permission. Fortunately, Father Müller had softened and granted George permission when he was considering missionary work in Bucharest, so now there was no resistance at a mere change in location. But George was lacking permission of another kind.

The Prussian government required from university graduates a year of service in the army. Most men leaving the country to do mission work were given a release from this duty, but despite several tries, George was not able to get one. Then another development loomed, threatening to further hinder his plans. George hadn't had good health in his late teens and early adulthood, having suffered several debilitating episodes of a serious nature, and problems struck again as he was waiting to get started with his missionary training. Feeling unwell on and off for a long period, his health suddenly took a sharp decline when he experienced bleeding in his stomach. He was in a weakened condition for some time, all the while waiting for a solution to the year of army service, and soon would be forced to report for active duty. A Christian friend who was a major in the army suggested George do just that — go for the army medical exam and see whether they came to the conclusion that he was not physically fit to join the service. This idea proved successful and George, who was truly unhealthy at the time, was declared unfit and exempted from all military duty. His health problems began to improve after a believing medical professor suggested he give up all the medicine he had been taking.

The way was now clear for travel to England to begin his work, but before leaving the country, George visited his father, who was now living back in Heimersleben. Sleeping again in the old house and walking those familiar streets caused George to think back to his wanton boyhood in that town. What a different person he was from the hopeless young man who was sent to prison. He now had a living hope, and grieved that so few in Heimersleben, including his family, knew of it themselves. He was anticipating another visit and further chances to talk to his father and brother after his six-month training, but circumstances didn't allow his return for quite some time.

George's channel-crossing was delayed a few weeks because of winter ice on the waterways in Rotterdam, still thick enough to prevent steamer travel. By the middle of March, the ice finally had cleared sufficiently, and George Müller was able to board his steamer, arriving in London 19 March 1829.

3

Paths in England

Rules and more rules! *This* is not allowed, and *that* may only be done by permission. George, not by nature a rule-follower, had never seen so many regulations. As a student in the mission seminary, George might have completely given up the idea of being a missionary to the Jews had he not reminded himself that submission to the rules was for the Lord's sake. And he loved his studies: Hebrew language, Chaldee, and the Rabbinic Alphabet. He prayed as he studied, asking for guidance and help, and felt he was making good progress, often working over his books twelve hours a day. His progress in the English language, however, was minimal. And no wonder — most of his fellow students were also German. He was feeling right at home with them, but they didn't offer much opportunity to practise the language of the land. One clear spring day while taking some fresh air, he came across a young boy in the fields, and thinking the lad wouldn't be too judgemental of his thick Prussian accent, struck up a conversation. What joy it gave him to communicate in English for the first time the good news of Jesus.

It was at this time that Müller first heard the remarkable story of a dentist from Exeter who was travelling to Persia with his wife and children, intending to be a missionary. He had given up his practice and a very comfortable salary, trusting God alone to provide for his needs — his name: Anthony Norris Groves. Inspired by the story, George jotted down some notes about it in his journal and even mentioned it in a letter to some friends in Prussia. It wouldn't be the last time the name Groves would come to his attention.

In the middle of May, George was reminded that not so long before he had been very ill — because the old trouble was back. Perhaps it was the long hours of study without much fresh air or exercise that weakened him again. This time was different, though, George being so sick he imagined his very life ebbing away. Far from being frightened, he felt a great peace, knowing his sins were forgiven, and was perfectly happy to slip into the arms of Jesus. His friends, however, were concerned: 'Please, George, you need to get a change of air to recover. Won't you consider going into the country for a while?' When his doctor agreed, George somewhat reluctantly left for the recommended location, Teignmouth (TIN-muth) in Devon, a few miles south of Exeter. As he was in the habit of doing before beginning any enterprise, he prayed. *Lord, please bless this journey to the benefit of my body and my soul.* His prayer couldn't have been more wonderfully answered.

It was there, where the River Teign empties into the English Channel, that George met Henry Craik, a young man from Scotland. They immediately discovered several things in common: they were the same age, they had both become

Christians while at university (Henry at St Andrews), and most importantly, they both were looking for a way to best serve their Saviour. Upon meeting this new friend, George also learned some interesting information: Henry had until just recently been the tutor for the children of Anthony Norris Groves, the dentist who gave up his practice to be a missionary in Persia.

While in Teignmouth, George attended a series of special worship services at the Ebenezer Chapel. He was impressed with one of the guest preachers, appreciating the solemnity in his treatment of the Bible, and had opportunity to spend ten days in the company of this man from London at the home of some Christian friends. Unfortunately, to the distress of his biographers and historians, Müller often neglected to provide names of family and other acquaintances in his private journals, and such was the case for this man who so inspired and blessed him regarding the ways of God and his Word.

'God began to show me,' he wrote, 'that His Word alone is our standard of judgement; that it can be explained only by the Holy Spirit; and that in our day, as well as in former times, He is the teacher of the people.' Müller put aside his commentaries and other books *about* the Bible, and began to read the book itself with prayer and meditation. This both excited and blessed him, and spurred him on to find more treasure for his heart and wisdom in his understanding. Studying the Bible anew in this way, George came to accept some truths, which from then on never wavered in his mind. He understood that the Holy Spirit is the one who shows a person the need for Christ and enables belief, that God the

Father chose his children from the foundation of the world, and that he will keep them safely his for ever. In the matter of the return of the Lord, he apprehended from his study that the world is not going to be universally converted before the second coming of Jesus, as he had previously been taught, but that Christians should be looking for his return at any time, just as the apostles did. (In later years he qualified this idea by teaching that a few events in history need to occur before the return.) And finally, he listed in his journal in the organized manner which he always employed, 'it ill becomes the servant to seek to be rich, and great and honoured in the world, when his Lord was poor, and mean, and despised.'

George Müller, at age twenty-four, was so greatly encouraged and inspired by the new light he was given that he counted it almost as a second conversion. He returned to London in the autumn with a new enthusiasm, beginning an early-morning Bible study with his fellow students at the mission seminary and, convinced he should preach the gospel as Jesus commanded, authorized missionary or not, began an evangelism ministry right there in the city. He passed out tracts, preached to groups of Jews where gathered together, read the Scriptures to a large meeting of Jewish boys, and taught Sunday school. He petitioned the Society to send him out in a field of work as soon as possible; but, receiving no answer, he began to pray about what his future work should be. The more he prayed, the more he felt that God himself knew better than the London Society where and when he should be working, and began to question whether the missionary society was the best place for him. Feeling he owed a debt to them, he offered himself without salary to preach where God might lead him.

During a winter break at the first of the year, George travelled to the home of some friends he had met the summer before in Exmouth and preached where he had opportunity. His English was much better by then, and he was well able to explain the truths from the Word of God that so excited him. It was at that time Müller's connection with the Society was mutually severed through correspondence, the mission society understandably unwilling to send out a worker who was not under their direction. As to the question of temporal support, George claimed the Bible's promises, among them Matthew 6, where Jesus says not to be anxious about bodily needs: 'But seek ye first the kingdom of God and his righteousness, and all these things will be added unto you.' He was also encouraged by the example of Dr Groves, who had already arrived in Baghdad to begin his missionary work.

After three weeks in Exmouth, George moved on again, looking for a place to preach, and thought to re-acquaint himself with friends in nearby Teignmouth. He was hoping for a chance to share the news of God's goodness to him recently and had in mind a visit of about ten days. His stay there turned out much differently than expected.

It just happened that the pastor of the Ebenezer Chapel was soon leaving, and one of the church members told Mr Müller, almost upon his arrival, that he wished he would become the new minister. This wasn't what George had in mind, and he explained: 'I don't intend to be stationary in any place, but to go through the country, preaching the Word as the Lord may direct me.' There were some in Teignmouth who, after hearing Mr Müller preach, agreed with him that he should keep on moving. 'My preaching there was ... disliked by many of the hearers...' he recorded. But others were touched by his messages, and some were very changed — converted. His presence stirred a great controversy, but George, not one to back away from a challenge and seeing that his messages were causing a number to search the Bible for themselves, determined to stay until he was asked to leave.

After twelve weeks, the eighteen people who composed the congregation unanimously asked George Müller to stay as the pastor, and he accepted their invitation, but gave notice that he would stay with them only as long as he 'saw it clearly to be the will of the Lord.' That spring of 1830 George Müller began his first pastorate, Ebenezer Chapel offering him a starting salary of fifty-five pounds a year, an amount that would provide adequately for his needs.

In addition to attending to his duties at Teignmouth, Pastor Müller often travelled to other towns to preach: Shaldon, Exmouth, Topsham and Exeter, among others. He challenged his listeners in each congregation to search the Scriptures, but once while visiting the little town of Sidmouth, some women of the church challenged *him*. When asked his opinion regarding baptism, he indicated that he had been baptized as an infant and felt no need of further baptism. 'Have you ever searched the Scriptures and prayed with reference to this subject?' one woman asked. George indicated truthfully that he had not. 'Then,' she said, 'I entreat you never to speak any more about it till you have done so.' At that point in time, after study, he decided in favour of baptism for confessing believers. He followed through, being baptized by immersion. Also that summer, Pastor Müller began the practice of holding the Lord's

Supper every week in his church, imitating the habit of the Apostles, who broke bread every Lord's Day.

A weekly preaching engagement was arranged for Pastor Müller in the little village of Poltimore, just outside Exeter, and as it was somewhat far from Teignmouth, overnight lodging was necessary. He was recommended a boarding school with extra rooms, Northernhay House, owned by a Mr and Mrs Hake. This Mrs Hake was an invalid who depended on the help of a capable and caring housekeeper — Mary Groves. She was the sister of Anthony Norris Groves, of whom George was already well aware, and after the first acquaintance, George often found reason to visit Exeter. Mary was almost eight years his senior, but he discovered in her a well-educated, musical and artistic woman, who, most importantly, was a devoted Christian with the same outlook on life as her brother — a trust and dependence on God.

Müller wrote in his journal at this time (tersely, as usual), that after prayer and deliberation he was convicted that it 'was better for me to be married'. It's probable that he was at least a bit more personal and passionate when he proposed to Mary by letter. Four days later, when George was at Northernhay House in person, she accepted and the two knelt in prayer to ask God's blessing — the first of thousands of times the couple would petition the Lord together. A new housekeeper was found for Mrs Hake, and on 7 October 1830 the two were married at a simple service in Exeter, beginning a union that was marked by happy and lasting compatibility. George chose well. Mary would prove to be perfectly qualified for the unique position she would hold as his wife.

Soon after the marriage, Müller came to the conviction that the method of providing his salary from pew rents was against the specific admonitions of Scripture and the 'mind of the Lord.' He cited James 2, verses 1-6, where the church was chastised for flattering the rich by giving them the best seats in the assembly, and dishonouring the poor by making them stand or sit on the floor. The old method of pew rents made the same distinction: the higher the rent, the better the seat. 'The Lord loveth a cheerful giver,' the Bible teaches, but when the collectors of the rents came around at specific times, it was difficult for some members to come up with the money and likely caused resentment and perhaps deprivation. For these reasons, George gave up his salary and told the congregation that if they had a desire to support him, they could give voluntary gifts. All seats in the chapel would be free, and a sign saying so was posted at the entrance. At the back of Ebenezer Chapel another addition appeared, a wooden box with a lock and a slot in which members could put their offerings.

Mary was in complete agreement with this decision about the pew rents, and there were more decisions to come. Müller was determined that he, from that time on, should never ask for any money, or indicate to any person that he was in need, and further, that they should obey the commandment of Jesus in Luke 12:

> 'Sell what ye have, and give alms; provide yourselves bags which grow not old, a treasure in the heavens that faileth not, where no thief approacheth, neither moth corrupteth. For where your treasure is, there will your heart be also.'

Virtually everything but the essentials in the Müller household was sold and the money given to the poor. Both George and Mary were of the same mind — they prayed for the grace to trust in God alone for their needs. Because of his promises, all they needed to do was to ask him.

Very soon after that, Müller's faith was tested. At morning prayers, he was brought to remember the 'state of our purse', and the fact that only eight shillings resided there. He petitioned God to provide, and only four hours later, as the couple was visiting a Christian woman in the area, she asked if they needed any money. Müller resisted the temptation to say *yes!* — and replied: 'I told the brethren, dear sister, when I gave up my salary, that I would for the future tell the Lord only about my wants.'

The woman protested that God had prodded her several times with the thought that she should give money to them. Müller was already mentally thanking God, but didn't tell this woman about their poor circumstances, thinking it might influence her giving. He left it to God and changed the subject, but before they left, the woman made sure George Müller had in his pocket what she was determined to give him.

The box at the chapel was supposed to be emptied every week by one of the men in the church, but often three to five weeks would go by before the Müllers were brought any money. One morning, when they had a friend and a relative staying in their home, the butter was completely gone, and only nine pence remained to their name. The money from the box hadn't been given to them for several weeks, but the

Müllers didn't reveal their financial situation to the guests, sparing them any discomfort. True to his commitment, George didn't ask any man for help, but made his petition to God, praying that he bring to the mind of the responsible party that the pastor and wife could use some money. The next morning, immediately after church, the gentleman in charge of the box uncharacteristically unlocked it there and then, handing George a good number of coins from inside. 'My wife and I couldn't sleep at all last night, thinking you might be in want of money,' he confessed. The needy couple 'praised the Lord heartily'.

The Müllers were thankful for God's encouragement to them while in Teignmouth, and how he always in some way provided what they needed, even though they were reduced to almost nothing on numerous occasions. People brought them meat and bread, money arrived in the mail, an unexpected wage was paid, money was put in the box and by other means the Müllers were provided with food on the table at every meal and money to pay every bill. Henry Craik was by then pastoring a church in the nearby town of Shaldon, and had also stopped pew rents in his church. His experience had been the same as the Müllers': God had supplied his every need.

Now and then George spoke at Henry's church as well as at others. He was resolved to take no money for preaching in these neighbouring churches, however, not wanting the listeners to get the idea he was there for financial gain. But some in those congregations were just as resolved that they would give monetary support to the Müllers. On one occasion, after Müller declined his gift, a man stuffed paper-wrapped coins in the visiting pastor's coat pocket and ran off before he could protest. During the visit to a congregation in Barnstaple, Mrs Müller found a sovereign hidden in her purse, and upon returning home and unpacking the luggage, she and her husband were amused to find more money hidden in the suitcase.

The Müllers were much loved by the churches they visited in the Devon region, but of course the Teignmouth congregation had special affection for them. After two years the church had grown from eighteen people to about fifty and was learning to trust God, just as their pastor was showing by example. The brothers and sisters were unaware, however, that their shepherd was praying about a call to new fields, most likely in the capacity of a travelling evangelist. On Sunday 15 April 1832, Müller reminded his congregation that when he had come to them from London two years before, he had agreed to stay only as long as the Lord would lead him. He felt they should be warned that he would be leaving in the near future. 'There was much weeping afterwards,' he wrote.

Müller had no definite plans about where he would next go. Henry Craik was in Bristol on a four-week evangelism visit and had written to his friend about joining him as there was much work to do and it was the type of ministry that suited Müller. George wrote back saying he would come if it was the Lord's will, having in mind a short preaching mission of a few days.

The plans were soon made to work in Bristol for ten days, and Müller left on 20 April. The pastors preached in two different chapels, Gideon and Pithay, to large audiences. There was good evidence of success, many confessing their need for Jesus, including a habitual drunk who, on the way to the 'public house', was waylaid by a friend suggesting they go and hear the 'foreigner' preach. At the Pithay chapel the young man was among the many who heard the gospel from Mr Müller and was 'completely altered'.

So well attended was the last night's meeting at the Gideon Chapel that many were turned away, with the balconies under the barrel-shaped ceiling more than full, and people sitting in the aisles, the pulpit stairs and the vestry. When it was time to leave the city, dozens of people with tears in their eyes begged Müller and Craik to stay. This, along with evidence that God had blessed every work the two pastors undertook with souls coming to faith in Jesus Christ, caused both to consider making Bristol their new ministry.

They were not willing to make permanent arrangements, however, until they had a chance to go home to Devon where they could pray and weigh their decision without undue influence from Bristol. If they could face the tears of their congregations and still be convinced of the will of God in having them move, they felt they should do so. It took only a few days back in Teignmouth for both men to decide that God was leading them as a team to work in the city of Bristol.

There were many sad goodbyes as the Müllers visited members of the congregation for the last time, but despite much sighing, the people understood that God had other plans for their pastor. None of them, though, would ever have guessed what providence would bring.

4

Roots in Bristol

The old gabled building known as St Peter's Hospital, a unique Bristol landmark, was more than five hundred years old when on 24 November 1940 a German bomb obliterated it. Not a hospital in the modern sense of the word, the building had been an institution for the needy, the aged, the infirmed, the insane and children. A less euphemistic word for the place would be 'workhouse'. Able-bodied residents were expected to work in trade for their room and board. For adult men at St Peter's in the year 1832, the work day was from 6.00am to 6.00pm, and the assignment was breaking up rock at the nearby Clifton Hot Springs.

The workhouse had been in operation in Bristol since 1696, the building having been previously owned by wealthy merchants. It was something of an architectural singularity, the half-timbered façade embedded with a riot of embellishments, and further adorned under the eaves with carvings of mythological satyrs, their gaze fixed on the neighbouring St Peter's Church. Inside, much of the ornate furnishings still remained after the building was converted to a workhouse, and was startling in juxtaposition to the crowded and unhealthy conditions there. By the year 1832, the building was overflowing — not only were all the beds full, but multiple sleepers huddled in each one. Six hundred people were applying for entrance.

Like other large cities in England, Bristol was suffering from growing pains. The changes in the nation's economy were increasing in their pace, small farmers being pushed off the land where holdings were enclosed into larger and more profitable agricultural operations, and families flocking to the cities in the hope of finding employment, some with their farm animals in tow. Once enjoying a golden age as the second largest of England's ports (unfortunately corresponding to the height of the slave trade), Bristol was not able to retain its position in the shipping industry, and unemployment was high. Many, though, preferred scraping by on the streets or even begging rather than living in the workhouse.

This was the city that Müller and Craik would now call home. George and Mary, along with her father, a widower, arrived by coach on 25 May 1832. Henry Craik joined them the next day, and the men spent several days seeking suitable lodgings for all four of them, with little success. After making it a subject of earnest prayer, they were given an answer in the form of a plain furnished house with three bedrooms, two sitting rooms, 'coals and attendance'. 'How good is the Lord to have thus appeared for us, in answer to prayer, and what an encouragement to commit every thing to him in prayer', Müller wrote, characteristically recognizing God's hand at work and delighting in it.

Gideon Chapel agreed to their requests that no pew rents be charged, and that, for the time, the two men have no fixed pastoral relationship with the church. As they had done before, the Müllers and Henry Craik would depend only on the Lord for their needs. A Christian man offered to pay the rent for a year in another location on Great George Street, the Bethesda Chapel, and so Müller and Craik took turns preaching at the two locations. On Sundays one congregation would hear Craik's Scottish brogue from the pulpit, and the other congregation listened to Müller's Prussian pronunciation of the language. But both men preached from the same book, the Word of God, and urged trust in the author. So many people wanted to talk further with their pastors about issues of the soul, that both men were kept busy counselling inquirers in the vestry at appointed afternoons and evenings during the week, the sessions often lasting several hours.

It should be mentioned, before proceeding, that this period in George Müller's life was a humbling one. A number in both the congregations preferred the preaching of Henry Craik to that of George Müller, and there were ways in which Craik's ministry was more outwardly effective. Müller was not unaware of the situation, but he harboured no envy for his brother, having a great admiration for his friend. He was content to take the less lofty position, knowing that the two of them working together could make up deficiencies that one alone might have, to the good of the ministry as a whole. But he was not content to do less than his best for God, and was challenged by Henry Craik's prayerfulness and concern for the unconverted.

One week after meetings began at Bethesda, the first case of cholera appeared in Bristol. The sickness spread quickly, cholera bacteria breeding in primitive sewage systems, seeping into water sources, polluting food, and clinging to unwashed hands. Cholera made virulent attack on the intestines, and most of those who became ill died of severe dehydration and subsequent shock, some within just a few hours. A woman a few doors down from the Müllers became sick at three in the morning and was dead by three in the afternoon.

By the middle of August the epidemic had spread throughout Bristol, and funeral bells were ringing almost continually, the community at a loss as to the true cause and treatment of the terrifying disease, most believing it came on from polluted vapours. Newspapers and pamphlets suggested all manner of dietetic and hygienic regimens, but at the Gideon Chapel the Great Physician was petitioned. A special 6.00am prayer meeting was organized, and every day up to three hundred people prayed for their friends and neighbours in the city of Bristol. Müller wrote of those times:

> *'The ravages of this disease are becoming daily more and more fearful. We have reason to believe that great numbers die daily in this city. Who may be the next, God alone knows. I have never realized so much the nearness of death. Except the Lord keep us this night, we shall be no more in the land of the living tomorrow ... into thy hands, O Lord, I commend myself!'*

The pastoral team was run ragged ministering to the sick day and night. One woman they visited, clearly not long for the world, was shrieking in such terrible discomfort they could hardly communicate. Müller felt as though the cholera was coming upon him there and then. Henry Craik managed to carve out some time to go and urge God's offer of love and salvation to those at the workhouse. Sadly, in a matter of a few weeks, scores of souls perished in the crowded conditions at St Peters.

George was also making fervent prayer at that time for his wife, who was pregnant and close to being due at the height of the epidemic. In his journal entry for 17 September, he wrote: 'This morning the Lord, in addition to all His other mercies, has given us a little girl, who, with her mother, are doing well.' The baby was named Lydia, after Mary's mother and also the youngest of her four sisters.

Two weeks later, the epidemic appeared to have run its course, and the churches at Gideon Chapel and Bethesda gave thanks that only one member had died of cholera. Some of those who attended the prayer meetings continued to be interested in the things of God and joined the worship services. The congregations were growing steadily under the care of the two young men — no one having any inkling as to the plans a small group of missionaries on another continent had for their pastors. In January 1833, both Müller and Craik received letters from Baghdad asking them to go and help in the missionary effort there. Drafts in the amount of two hundred pounds accompanied the letters, to cover the costs of travel to Persia. From the consternation this event provoked, it seems sure that the letters from Dr Groves and other brethren in Baghdad were unexpected. It was time for George Müller to pray again about the call to the mission field. He had no preconceived idea about how God would answer his prayer and spent hours petitioning for clarity. The question was up in the air for over two weeks, but in the end neither Müller nor Craik perceived God leading them to leave the ministry they had in front of them.

Müller took stock of the progress in Bristol after the first year. Bethesda Chapel, which started with only a handful of people, had grown to sixty in number, and Gideon Chapel had gained forty-nine. As far as they could count, the number of conversions was sixty-five, and 'many backsliders have been reclaimed, and many of the children of God have been encouraged and strengthened in the way of truth. What clear proofs that we were not suffered to be mistaken, as it regards our coming to Bristol', wrote Müller.

Most of the church members in Bristol were poor, and their distress grieved Mr Müller. It pained him even more to see boys and girls, men and women in the streets, who were constantly hungry. That winter he had begun to read the journal of August Hermann Francke, founder of the large orphanage where he had stayed as a student in Halle, and was reminded that Francke had begun his work with children by feeding the poor outside his back door. 'The Lord graciously help me to follow him, as far as he followed Christ', prayed George. The Müllers began to feed people at their own back door every day. (This was also Henry Craik's back door since Craik and Müller were still sharing a home.) The more people who came for bread, the more money was given by others to provide for them. Thirty or forty were gathering regularly.

A. H. Francke recorded that he began to invite the poor into his home for a short period of religious instruction. This excerpt from Francke's journal in 1694 couldn't have escaped Müller's attention:

It seemed a great shame to the Christian name that so many people should grow up like cattle, without any knowledge of divine things, and especially that so many children, in consequence of the poverty of their parents, should neither be sent to school, nor enjoy good training at home, but grow up in the most scandalous ignorance and vice...

George Müller shared the same sentiments as Francke, though in a different country and almost one hundred and forty years later. His thoughts in June 1833 turned to the idea of finding a nearby location that would be appropriate to gather a large group of people, to distribute food, and to instruct both children and adults in reading and the Bible. He conferred with Henry Craik and began to make plans, but because of overwhelming pastoral duties at that point, the idea had to be put on hold.

God was blessing Müller and Craik both in their work and in their temporal needs, as they continued to depend only on him for their provision. George recorded the gifts and his thankfulness:

June 22. A brother sent a hat to brother Craik and one to me, as a token of his love and gratitude, like a thank-offering as he says. This is now the fourth hat which the Lord has kindly sent me successively, whenever, or even before I needed one. Between August 19th and 27th was sent to us, by several

*individuals a considerable quantity of fruit. How kind of the
Lord, not merely to send us the necessities of life, but even
such things as, on account of the weakness of our bodies, or
the want of appetite, we might have desired.*

The people gathering at the Müllers' back door grew to an
even larger number, and neighbours began to complain
of beggars loitering on the street all day. That summer it
became necessary to stop the practice of feeding the poor
at his home, but Müller didn't forget about his desire to
somehow help the destitute with instruction in reading and,
more importantly, to share his faith in Jesus.

In February 1834, Müller was suffering a spiritual lethargy.
The honest entries in his journal bemoaned the coldness in
his love for God and cried out to him for improvement in
his spiritual life: '...I cannot be satisfied with such a state of
heart. Oh that once more I might be brought to fervency
of spirit, and that thus it might continue with me for ever!
... within the last week I have repeatedly set out, as it were,
afresh, but soon, very soon, all has come again to nothing.
The Lord alone can help me.' On 21 February, he recorded
God's answer to his prayer: 'Through the help of the Lord
I am in rather a better state of heart than for some time
past. I was led this morning to form a plan for establishing,
upon scriptural principles, an institution for the spread of
the Gospel at home and abroad. I trust this is a matter of
God.' Twelve days later both Müller and Craik, convinced
of the rightness of the idea and of God's blessing, publicly
presented the plans for the new organization, bearing the
perfectly descriptive but cumbersome name of 'Scriptural
Knowledge Institution for Home and Abroad.'

5

Germination of a new work

If George Müller had done nothing more in his life than establishing and promoting the 'Scriptural Knowledge Institution for Home and Abroad', his work would have been deemed remarkable and substantial. Its help and influence reached far and wide for the kingdom of Christ. The goals of the organization at its inception were multi-faceted, but all pointed to the broadcast of God's Word.

The first purpose was to help support existing Sunday schools and day schools for children, and to begin, as God allowed, schools of their own where all the teachers would be Christians. Schools for teaching adults how to read and study the Bible would also be in the plan.

Central to the organization would be the widespread distribution of Bibles, the second aim of the institution. The intent was to obtain large quantities of publications at a good price so that they might be sold at a reduced rate, making them accessible to those with low incomes. In cases of extreme want, the Bibles would be given away.

The third goal involved the 'Abroad' aspect of the organization. Financial and other support would be given to missionaries who were faithfully spreading God's Word in other countries.

Equally important to the goals of the institution were the methods that should be used to implement them. Under no circumstances was the institution to go into debt, but it was to work within the means God would give, supplied after secret prayer. The patronage of unbelievers would not be sought out, nor funds solicited of them, and non-Christians would never be used to manage or implement affairs of the organization.

Two weeks after the eventful first meeting of the new institution, a new member was born into the Müller family, a little boy, unnamed for more than a month. After much discussion, and then prayer, George decided on the name Elijah. With an infant in the house in addition to little Lydia, George, Mary, her father, and the growing Craik family (Henry was now married with one child), the Müllers decided they should look for a place of their own.

They were blessed with a new home at Number 21 Paul Street, an address that would long be associated with the Müllers and a welcoming haven for friends and relatives. It was the end dwelling in a row of plain four-storeyed houses, with nine steps in front and a garden at the back. Some Christian friends kindly donated money for furniture, and carpet was given to make the home comfortable.

Along with the move, Müller was busy at work for the Institution. In July he recorded that he spent much time in prayer for a master of a boys' school, as he had interviewed eight candidates who were all unsuitable. At last, his prayers were answered with a qualified teacher. The next month George reported that he and Henry had hired a governess for a girls' school. Opportunities and funding kept flowing in so that by the autumn, only seven months after the Institution was begun, there were forty students in the school for adults, one hundred and twenty children in the Sunday schools, and two hundred and nine children in the four day schools begun by the Institution — two for boys and two for girls. Four hundred and eighty-two Bibles had been distributed, five hundred and twenty New Testaments, and fifty-seven pounds had been sent to help missionaries. In all, the total tabulated giving to the Scriptural Knowledge Institution 'as the fruit of many prayers', was 167 pounds, 10 shillings and one-half pence.

One might visualize George recording this in delight, after carefully consulting his detailed bookkeeping, much like the accounts his father had kept in Heimersleben. He was painstaking, cautious to correctly assign donations as they were intended by the giver, whether they were for the Institution, church or for personal use.

In addition to the administrative duties of the Institution and his ministry in the chapels, George happily took on a new area of work — speaking to the children in their schools about the Lord. It's not recorded how often Müller was able to do this, but we do know at least one result of his visits. A young lad, likely one of a number of the children who were granted free tuition, had responded to Pastor Müller's teaching with a concern for his soul. Müller was very much affected when told of what happened to the boy after that. He was an orphan and, having no other place to live, was forced to move 'some miles from Bristol' to a workhouse, sadly unable to continue attending school.

In many cases, orphaned children were taken in by relatives. This was a burden to families already marginally surviving, especially if there were numerous children, as was often the case. Those orphans who had no family to care for them were sent to the workhouse, the only other option for parentless children in Bristol. There were few homes specifically for orphans in the whole of England, and those that existed required personal recommendations for admission, or sufficient votes among the board of trustees. Only children of respectable upper- or middle-class families were considered.

The year before, in 1834, residents from the overrun St Peter's Hospital had been transferred to a larger set of buildings at Stapleton, two miles from Bristol, the likely destination of the lad from the school. It was in that year that a new group of national poor relief laws had been enacted, intending to consolidate and economize the support of the poor, with the number of needy approaching a crisis level. Aid was not to be given except to those who applied at a workhouse, and the parishes were advised to make the conditions there less preferable than those of the lowest paid labourer, the calculated deprivation serving as a deterrent to those who in any way could work. These were the institutions where the orphans were sent to live. They shared their lives with the aged, the sick, and the insane, subsisting on a poor diet in dreary overcrowded accommodations rampant with disease. Müller was pained when he considered the lot of the poor orphan boy who was sent away, and observed the awful conditions of the droves of children in his city who had no one to care for them.

In the early months of 1835, missionaries again gained his attention. Dr Groves was looking for new workers to go to Calcutta, and Müller, always willing to assist in the spread of the gospel, agreed to help translate and preach on a recruiting tour through Germany and Switzerland. Dr Groves was holding out hope that his sister's husband might be convinced to join in the mission venture himself. This was not to happen, George having his own personal mission on the trip. He was looking forward to seeing his father and brother again in Heimersleben, having prayed for them since leaving Prussia, and was in deep concern for their souls.

The five-week trip was gruelling, but successful. One of the high points for Müller proved to be his visit to Halle, where he saw the old places that were so much part of his early Christian life and the friends he held so dear, including the warmhearted Dr Tholuck. He was also well received by his father, and although no particular interest in the gospel was shown, there was no direct resistance. 'May God help me to follow your example, and act according to what you have said to me,' he told George at the end of his visit.

The summer of that year was the most difficult the Müllers had ever faced. God, for his own reasons, allowed the family to go through a time of sorrows, with serious illness coming to the house. The two Müller children and their grandfather, Mr Groves, all became sick. Mr Groves became ill first and was overcome by the infection, dying on 22 June. Three days later, fifteen-month-old Elijah, who had become much sicker than Lydia, was struggling for every breath. Pneumonia, which in modern times is often easily cured, was choking the life out of the littlest Müller. 'The dear little boy is so ill, that I have no hope of his recovery,' Müller wrote on 25 June. Earnest prayer was made that God would spare the child of any more suffering. The couple left their little son's life in God's hands, and Elijah did not linger. He became one of the multitudes of youngsters to fall victim to a fast-moving infection, the grief no less to the families though the anguish frequent. From all records, it is probable the Craik family suffered the loss of several of their little ones.

Müller's further prayers were for Mary — for God's support of his grief-stricken wife, who had lost both father and son within one week. He was given great comfort as he thought about his little one in the care of Jesus, who loved the boy even more than his parents. 'When I weep, I weep for joy,' wrote Müller, perfectly assured that his child was happier in the bosom of the Lord than he was in the world.

George Müller spent his thirtieth birthday (27 September) on the Isle of Wight. This was no celebratory vacation, however, the reason for the change of air being another debilitating illness. Not having the physical strength to work was a test of his patience and depressing in spirit. 'Today I am thirty years of age,' he wrote. 'I feel myself an unprofitable servant.' It wasn't the sea air that lifted his spirits, but time spent in refreshing prayer that began to set him on the road to recovery.

As his health improved, Müller was encouraged by reading a biography of John Newton, the slave trader who was saved from a life of depraved callousness and found by God. This inspired Müller to weigh up an idea: 'October 9. I have many times had thoughts of giving in print some account of the Lord's goodness to me, for the instruction, comfort and encouragement of the children of God; and I have been more than ever stirred up to do so since I read Newton's life a few days ago. I have considered, today, all the reasons for and against, and find that there are scarcely any against, and many for it.' In the following weeks he began writing as he had opportunity.

The Müllers returned to Bristol in the middle of October, George ready to take on the work waiting for him. He would need all the strength God would give him because the next month, November 1835, he took a momentous step. Müller would remember that time clearly for the rest of his life, and credited God for his direct leading. It began when a woman offered him tea in her home. While Pastor Müller waited for his cup of tea, the English translation of the little book of August Hermann Francke, sitting on a shelf among others, caught his attention. Two years before, the autobiography had inspired Müller to think about what he could do for the poor in Bristol, and now the story of the large orphan home in Halle where he once lived was put again in front of him. He didn't consider it a coincidence. He recorded the circumstances in his journal, seeming so ordinary upon casual reading: 'November 20: This evening I took tea at a sister's house where I found Francke's life. I have frequently, for a long time thought of labouring in a similar way, though it might be on a much smaller scale, not to imitate Francke, but in reliance upon the Lord. May God make it plain!'

Three days later, Müller received money in the mail for the Scriptural Knowledge Institution, which was an answer to prayer for specific needs. He had asked God for forty pounds, and the money from the mail brought the total received to almost fifty pounds. God could provide from his vast storehouse whatever the need, Müller decided, whether it was for the Institution, or for orphans.

The next two weeks he thought about little else but the possibility of beginning an orphan work, and the underlying reasons to begin such a venture. It all came down to giving glory to God and strengthening the faith of believers. 'Seek ye first the kingdom of God, and his righteousness and all these things will be added unto you,' he would remind his brothers and sisters in the congregation. But they fretted and worried, working too many hours, feeling forced to be employed in occupations unsuitable to believers and sometimes even using shady business practices to increase the family income. Müller pointed out that 'their Heavenly Father always helps those who put their trust in him'. He was convinced they needed proof, visible proof that God had not changed, and could be taken at his word. He later wrote of his reasoning:

> Now if I, a poor man, simply by prayer and faith, obtained, without asking any individual, the means for establishing and carrying on an Orphan-House; there would be something which with the Lord's blessing might be instrumental in strengthening the faith of the children of God besides being

a testimony to the consciences of the unconverted, of the reality of the things of God. This, then, was the primary reason, for establishing the Orphan-House. I certainly did from my heart desire to be used by God to benefit the bodies of poor children, bereaved of both parents, and seek, in other respects, with the help of God to do them good for this life; I also particularly longed to be used by God in getting the dear orphans trained up in the fear of God but still, the first and primary object of the work was (and still is) that God might be magnified by the fact, that the orphans under my care are provided with all they need, only by prayer and faith, without any one being asked by me or my fellow-labourers, whereby it may be seen, that God is FAITHFUL STILL and HEARS PRAYER STILL... (capitals per Müller)

He recorded in his journal several days in a row the supplication at God's throne regarding this new venture. *Take every thought of this out of my mind, if it not be of You,* Müller prayed. He consulted with Henry Craik and John Corser, an Anglican clergyman who had given up his position to help Müller's work in Bristol. (Craik had been in ill health for some time and, because of throat problems, even had to give up preaching for some months.) He searched his heart for any self-gratifying motives, and finally decided that the only objection to the work was that his other duties in the church and the Scriptural Knowledge Institution already kept him more than busy. If the plan was of God, he would provide the help, George reasoned, and perhaps the orphan home wouldn't take too much of his time.

Müller's final conclusion was that the work was too important to ignore or put off, and he arranged to have handbills printed for a meeting on 9 December. As he was anticipating the special gathering of supporters of the Scriptural Knowledge Institution, he was struck by a verse in his Bible reading on the evening of 5 December: 'Open thy mouth wide and I will fill it,' (Psalm 81:10). He interpreted this verse as urging him to ask God for the whole scope and sum of needs to begin an orphan home. A practical man, he sat down and computed what the needs would be: a place of lodging for the children, suitable caretakers, and at least 1,000 pounds. He wouldn't ask God for a taste of blessing, but a huge helping, and his provision would confirm that the house for orphans was his will.

The evening of 9 December Müller stood before the supporters of the Scriptural Knowledge Institution for Home and Abroad and explained his proposal for the orphan home. 'It will only be established if the Lord should provide both the means for it, and suitable persons to conduct it. As to the means, I would make the following remarks. The reason for proposing to enlarge the field, is not because we have of late particularly abounded in means, for we have been rather straitened...' He proposed using the same operating procedures of the Institution if the Lord desired the home to be established — incurring no debts and using only Christian workers. It would be open free of charge to any child who had lost both parents. No offering was taken that night, but the next day Müller had published in the local newspaper a summary of the considered plans and stated that believers wishing to make donations of household items and children's clothing or fabric could be assured the items would be thankfully received at his home.

6

Fruits of vision and prayer

George Müller carefully penned in his journal: '...ten basins, eight mugs, one plate, five dessert spoons, six teaspoons, one skimmer, one toasting fork, one flour dredge [shaker], one pillow case, one table cloth; also one pound.'

The stream of donations had begun, and George was encouraged by each one, thanking God as he recorded them. The members of his own two congregations were, for the most part, barely getting by financially — not in a position to give any more out of their incomes, but Müller was confident God could supply from other sources. He installed a box at his home for orphan house donations and, nearly every day, gifts of money or of some other kind came in. Some donors gave more substantially than an extra item or two from their household. Fifty pounds were donated by a person from whom Müller would never have expected such a sum. A woman offered herself to work in the home immediately after the meeting, and the next day he received a letter from a brother and sister who wrote: 'We propose ourselves for the service of the intended Orphan-House, if you think us qualified for it; also to give up all the furniture etc., which the Lord has given us, for its use; and to do this without receiving any salary whatever, believing, that if it be the will of the Lord to employ us He will supply all our need...'

Whenever Müller wondered if the final goal could be achieved, or if God's hand was in the project, he'd pray for encouragement — and it was sent. 'This evening some one rang our house bell,' recorded George. 'When the door was opened, no one was there, but a kitchen [fireplace] fender and a dish were found at the door, which, no doubt, were given for the Orphan-House.'

One woman, who was frail in health and earned very little as a seamstress, gave the astonishing sum of 100 pounds. George visited her, concerned she was acting on a temporary generous impulse, giving away money she would herself need later. He tried to talk her out of the gift, which came as part of an inheritance from her grandmother, making sure she wouldn't in time regret her decision, but she insisted: 'The Lord Jesus has given His last drop of blood for me, and should I not give Him this 100 pounds?' In the end, she had her way, and insisted Müller take another five pounds for the poor in the church.

By the final days of January, it was determined that sufficient support had come in to begin taking applications for orphans. Young girls were seen as having the greatest need for shelter and protection, and so thirty girls aged seven to twelve would be accepted into the new home, with

3 February the assigned day to put in application. Müller waited expectantly that morning in the vestry of Gideon Chapel, hoping to compile a list of names and ages of the prospective residents and perhaps getting a chance to meet some of them. But he left for home at lunch time, dejected that not one application was made. When it occurred to him that he had prayed to God for everything about the new orphan home except the children who were to live there, he was devastated. Müller didn't consider this a mere inadvertent oversight. He asked the Lord for forgiveness in presuming upon him and not realizing that without his blessing in everything, the plans would surely fail. He spent the evening humbly re-examining his motives, and finally felt peace to pray for applications.

The next day the first one came in, and others followed in a steady stream. There were enough funds to rent a large three-storey brick building close to the Gideon Chapel, Number 6 Wilson Street. A matron to oversee the running of the home and a governess to instruct and shepherd the girls were selected, and work on the furnishings began. Mary, with the company of three-year-old Lydia, put in long hours sewing clothing, preparing furnishings and organizing the accounts. Other friends helped, and the donations kept coming in: blankets, bonnets, washbasins and jugs, kettles and saucepans, pinafores, hymnbooks and on and on. By 11 April, every bed was made, every dresser was filled and the kitchen was fully equipped — it was time for the first group of girls to arrive.

One of them was ten-year-old Harriet Culliford. Both of her parents had died of tuberculosis the year before, and there were no relatives or friends to give her a permanent home. She was nervous and excited as she walked through the rooms of the home at Number 6 Wilson Street for the first time. More girls would be coming in the next few days, but sadly her little sister, Leah, would not be among them, as she was one year short of the age requirement of seven years.

A special day of prayer and thanksgiving was held on 21 April, with seventeen girls now living in the house. Pastor Müller had met each one and knew them all by name. In the morning Pastor Craik spoke to the children and visitors, and in the afternoon all the children from the day schools, Sunday schools and the orphan home joined together at the chapel to hear Pastor Müller give a message from the Bible.

The beds weren't quite all occupied at Number 6 Wilson Street before a plan was made to open another home, this one for younger children: infants and boys and girls up to age six. Many applications had been put in previously for children younger than seven, and Müller reasoned that it would better to have the orphans taken in as soon as possible, before any moral or spiritual damage could be done while under temporary care. Harriet's little sister Leah was in the first group of residents at Number 1 Wilson St, just a few doors down from the girls' home in the block of adjoining houses. Müller was pleased to find such suitable accommodation, and happy to also secure a play-yard nearby. Müller wrote of the arrangements: 'How evident is the hand of God in all these matters! How important to leave our concerns, great and small, with Him; for He arranges all things well! If our work be His work, we shall prosper in it.'

Opening day was 28 November, just seven months after the girls' home was dedicated.

A few of the older and more capable girls were chosen to help with the infant orphans down at the new home. This helped to save the expense of hiring assistants, provided the older girls with experience in nursery care, and allowed them to stay longer in the girls' home by giving them built-in employment. The assignment was not an onerous one. With pink scrubbed cheeks and dressed in ruffled and embroidered hand-me-down gowns, the little orphans were as appealing as the original wearers of the frocks. Some of the baby clothing had come from the congregation in Teignmouth, who had not forgotten their pastor, and along with the clothing had sent collected funds.

Each year at the end of December Müller customarily entered in his journal a numerical summary: the number of souls added to both Gideon and Bethesda Chapels, and those who died, or for other reasons were no longer a part of the fellowship. In 1836, the total number fellowshipping in the two churches was 349. Completely transparent regarding his personal finances, he also recorded yearly what was given to him from the boxes at the church, in monetary presents, through family connections, and the value of gifts in goods. That year the total was 232 pounds, 11 shillings, and 9 pence (as near as he could determine).

Gifts earmarked for the orphan homes continued to flow in, and Müller carefully tabulated each pound, shilling and penny. In December 1835 he had prayed to the Lord for accommodation and staff for the orphan home and 1,000 pounds to start the work. The accommodation and staff had been provided, but the 1,000-pound goal had not yet been reached, though the two homes were able to open with less than the asked-for amount. Müller never forgot a prayer request. He was looking and waiting for those last pounds to come in, careful never to ask any individual for money towards this so that 'the Lord's hand might be seen in this matter.' Not only was he waiting to see God's hand, but he was looking forward to recording the blessing in his soon-to-be completed book, *A Narrative of Some of the Lord's Dealings with George Müller*. Even as he was finishing this narrative of his life, he prayed and agonized over the decision to publish. Would his autobiography join the abundant collection of superfluous religious books then in circulation?

In June 1837 there was cause for praise. After eighteen months and ten days God had sent the last of the money to make up the 1,000 pounds. Also that month there was both widespread mourning and grandiose celebration. In the early hours of 20 June King William IV died, and before the sun was above the horizon, Princess Victoria, in dressing gown and slippers, was saluted as queen of the United Kingdom. Four days later a group of officials paraded through the city of Bristol, its church bells ringing, and its citizens cheering at the streetsides, waving Union Jack flags in honour of their new queen. She was only eighteen years old and her reign, the Victorian era, would last beyond the lifetime of George Müller.

That summer the faithful Müller, with trust born of all God's previous provisions, and not daunted by the fact that there were two homes full of orphans with daily needs, had confidence to ask for more. The young boys at the Infant Home who were turning seven had no place to go, and there were still many homeless orphan boys on the streets. It was obvious to him that another home was needed for boys aged seven to fourteen, but Müller had neither time nor energy to juggle more responsibilities. He prayed for a brother to act as a steward to help him in his many duties, a pious master for the boys, someone to help care for their needs, and money enough to furnish a house and clothe forty boys. He would wait and see if the requests would be met, determining God's will in the matter.

While Müller waited for God's provision to start a third home, he cast his memory back over the five years he had been in Bristol and decided his blessings had been 'many and great, my trials few and small'. True to form, he listed out the many mercies and joys God had given to him, his congregations, and his friend Henry Craik during their time in that city. Among the blessings he listed the six Day Schools, the Sunday school, the Adult School, the 4,030 copies of Scripture circulated, the missionary support that was sent to India, Canada and Europe, and the sixty-four orphans who were now living in the homes. With those last thoughts, and two paragraphs to the reader, he sent his manuscript, *A Narrative of Some of the Lord's Dealings with George Müller*, to the printer. While he was proof-reading for final press, and just in time to include in the text, a single donor gave him four hundred and sixty pounds for the orphan work.

By autumn of that year, God had answered all of Müller's requests regarding the boys' orphan home except for the location. A house thought to be perfect was later given up when the neighbours objected to having so many children living next to them. Then Number 3 Wilson Street, between the other two homes, was offered for the boys, and gladly agreed upon. About this time, the first legacy for the orphans was received, from a young boy himself. The lad was very ill and, knowing his end was near, asked that the few coins he had in his little savings, 6 shillings and 6½ pence, should be given to the orphans.

All was nearly ready to open the boys' home, but Müller would have to depend upon the Lord and his helpers to see to the final details and welcome the boys. He had become incapacitated. One night in November he woke up with a 'weakness' in his head which only improved with a handkerchief tied tightly around his forehead. Finally able to get back to sleep, he was distressed that the symptoms were still there in the morning, and, as it turned out, for many weeks to come. He had difficulty concentrating, tired easily, and sometimes found himself regretfully irritable. Thanks to the generosity of Christian friends and acquaintances, he was able to get away from Bristol, seeking that change of air that might make some difference in his health. He was hardly able to hold a conversation, much less preach or handle administrative duties that had been steadily mounting.

First he travelled to Bath, where the symptoms became even more disturbing — in fact, Müller feared he was on the verge of insanity. No better when he got home, he and the family left for a stay at Weston-Super-Mare. Upon return to Bristol after ten days, Müller was much assured to hear from his doctor that he was in no danger of losing his mind, though the nerves of his head were likely in a 'disordered state'. Still not able to preach, or even attend church, Müller was given providential encouragement one Sunday when he was again homebound. Glancing out the window on the morning of 17 December, he saw a row of thirty-two girls walking on the street and immediately recognized them.

> *When I saw these dear children in their clean dresses, and their comfortable warm cloaks, and when I saw them walking orderly under the care of a sister to the chapel, I felt grateful to God that I had been made the instrument of providing for them, seeing that they are all better off, both as it regards temporal and spiritual things, than if they were at the places from whence they were taken. I felt that, to bring about such a sight, was worth the labour not only of many days, but of many months, or years. I felt that it answered all the arguments of some of my friends who say 'you do too much.'*

Müller was still ill after Christmas, but prepared the annual report for 1837, recording that there were eighty-one children at the three homes, with nine full-time staff. Applications for orphan care were still coming in, enough older girls seeking entrance to fill another home of thirty. Younger children were being turned away from the infant home for lack of room. 'Truly this is a large field of labour!' he wrote.

Continuing to suffer troubling symptoms in the new year of 1838, he was advised by his doctor to again get a change of air, and the Müller family travelled to Trowbridge to try the atmosphere there. While he was in Trowbridge, Müller read the life of George Whitefield, the eighteenth-century 'Great Awakening' evangelist of Britain and America, and was deeply impressed with the man's regular habit of reading the Bible in a prayerful posture on his knees. This he resolved to do, and was able, though far from having his full strength, to read and pray over Psalm 63 for two hours: 'O God, thou art my God, early will I seek thee, my soul thirsteth for thee, my flesh longeth for thee in a dry and thirsty land...' As he continued reading through the book of Psalms that week, he came to chapter 68, verse 5, where God is called a 'father to the fatherless.' 'By the help of God,' Müller wrote, 'this shall be my argument before Him respecting the orphans in the hour of need. He is their Father, and, therefore, has pledged Himself, as it were, to provide for them, and to care for them; and I have only to remind Him of the need of these poor children, in order to have it supplied.' He used this biblical appeal to God in prayer many times in the years that were to come.

Müller's health problem, which had now been diagnosed as an 'inactive liver', continued through the spring, occasioning travel to Bath, Oxford, Lutterworth and Leamington. At Oxford, he thought to try therapeutic horse exercise, which was touted by many in those days as a cure for almost anything. The ailing but determined Müller rode for three days on a seemingly compatible horse, but was prevented further exercise because the animal himself became ill. After a few days the horse was deemed better, but when Müller mounted up, the previously calm horse revealed a completely different personality: self-willed and skittish and impossible to ride. This was his last recorded equestrian experience.

It was about this time that Müller was asked of some missionaries to go once again to Germany, for another recruiting tour. He reasoned a trip to his native country might be restorative to his health, and he longed to see his father and brother again in Heimersleben. When his constitution was judged to be stable enough, the trip was approved by his doctor, and Henry Craik was agreeable to the plan. Müller left in April, and upon return from the month-long visit, his strength was increasing. On 8 May he was able to participate in public worship at Bethesda Chapel for the first time since November of the previous year.

He was glad for improvement in his health, but came back to Bristol saddened at the physical decline of his father, and the fact that his brother was living in 'open sin'. His prayer was that the words he spoke to them might have some convicting effect on their souls, unsure he would have another chance to see their faces again. As it happened, he visited Heimersleben once again the following February, finding his father much weaker than before. Affectionate to his son, Herr Müller had begun the habit of reading prayers and the Bible, but George could see no definite signs of a change in heart. He continued in ardent prayer for him, but was not able to see an answer for himself. His father passed away a month after the visit.

7

Drought and showers

'I have not one penny in hand for the orphans,' Müller wrote
on 18 August 1838. 'In a day or two again many pounds
will be needed. My eyes are up to the Lord.' Expenses were
well met in the first two years of the Bristol orphan work,
but difficult times now appeared on the horizon. On that
particular day, before evening, a woman who knew nothing
of the dire situation brought in five pounds. She had been
praying, and the thought came to her: *I have five pounds
extra right now, not owing it to anyone, and since I was going
to sell some of my jewellery for the orphans in time, why not
take the five pounds to them at once instead of waiting to
dispose of the trinkets?*

Two days later the money had run out again, and George
prayed. A lady who was staying in nearby Clifton, and whom
he had never met, sent twelve pounds. But circumstances
continued to be strained, with only small gifts coming in.
On 10 September, funds were again so low that Müller
recorded it as a 'solemn crisis'. The children were never to

know of these situations, and most of the workers up to that time were unaware of financial difficulties. However, at this point, he revealed to the staff at each home the crisis, asking what their expenses were at the time, advising them to avoid spending money on anything but basic needs, and requesting they let him know of any surplus articles in the homes that could be sold for cash. 'I still believe that God will help,' he told them, praying with the staff of each house, and then later with his friend Henry Craik.

There was money in the bank, 220 pounds to be exact, given to him for other Christian endeavours, but he wouldn't use that, trusting that God would provide a solution without his borrowing from designated funds. Neither would he buy supplies on credit, though it would have been gladly extended to him. For Müller, debt was to be avoided at all costs, and considering the position in which some Christian orphan home directors found themselves, this was a wise policy (both George Whitefield in Georgia, and later, Doctor Barnardo of London, fell into debt, to the detriment of their orphan work and their own reputations). There were those who had said to Müller, 'Tell me if you need any more money,' but he never took up any such offer and did his best to inform his donors that he would only rely on God to send what was needed. He could honestly say, in all his years of work for the Institution and the orphan homes, that no individual had ever been asked for money, and that God had been the one to supply the needs.

God did supply the needs at that time of solemn crisis. While Müller was praying at home mid-morning, a woman came to call and gave Mary two sovereigns for the orphans.

'I felt stirred up to come and have already delayed too long,' she explained to her. While she was still there, Müller came into the room, and the woman gave him another two sovereigns without him informing her of the financial straits. A few days later, a staff member approached him after a prayer time, with sixteen shillings in hand saying, 'It wouldn't be upright for me to pray if I didn't give what I had.' Müller accepted the donation with thanks. That week two other workers had donated some of their books to be sold, and one sold his watch for the orphans. Generosity on the part of the workers in lean times frequently helped make up shortages and demonstrated their selfless dedication to the support of the children in their care. Some of the staff laboured for no salary at all, and the rest of them agreed to the arrangement that their salary would be paid as it was supplied by the Lord. 'What a blessing to have such fellow-labourers!' Müller wrote at that time.

Müller's personal giving to the orphan work and to the missions of the Scriptural Knowledge Institution was remarkable. For years in the annual reports, frequent and generous gifts were recorded as being given by 'a servant of the Lord Jesus, who, constrained by the love of Christ, seeks to lay up treasure in heaven'. After his death, these donations were confirmed as being from Müller himself, a grand total of 81,490 pounds, 18 shillings and 8 pence from his own income — those monies given to him for personal use. Considering that the annual earnings of most people were well below 100 pounds a year, this was a huge amount.

The orphan work was also being supported sacrificially by many in the community at large. In December 1838, heavily attended meetings on three consecutive evenings were held to acquaint the public with the progress of the orphan homes and of the Scriptural Knowledge Institution for Home and Abroad. Despite the recent financial constraints, Müller remarked that God had provided for every need, and that, in general, the children were thriving, many improving in health since they had been in the homes. And also, that 'though most of them had been brought up in a very different manner from what one could desire, yet God has constrained them, on the whole, to behave exceedingly well, so much so that it has attracted the attention of all observers'.

On a bitter-sweet note at those same meetings, he told of God's mercy towards two little orphan girls whose parents had both died of consumption. The sisters were likely already suffering effects of the deadly disease themselves when they entered the homes. These were the same little girls introduced previously — Harriet Culliford being one of the first residents of the girls' home, and her sister, Leah, coming at the opening of the Infant Home. Harriet was nursed for many months by the caring staff, but showed no interest at all in the things of the Lord, nothing making an impression upon her. At last, about two weeks before she departed, the love and prayers for her bore fruit, and she gave her heart to Jesus, joyful at the prospect of being soon with him. Leah, who was about eight, 'fell asleep in Jesus' in the autumn of that year, showing every sign that she also was trusting in her Saviour. Müller declared that these events were an 'especial reason to rejoice'.

On 9 November 1839, Müller wrote: 'Not one penny was in hand.' 20 November: 'This has been a day of deep poverty.'

2 May 1840: 'Nothing having come in for five days, we were today again penniless.' 5 November 1840: 'We are now, without anything, cast upon the Lord.' 26 January 1842: 'Again there was nothing in hand when the day commenced.' Despite public interest, hard times periodically came upon the work, especially between the years of 1838–1843.

Was George Müller feeling the stress of frequently living so close to the edge of want? Did the weight of the responsibility in providing the necessities for dozens of children and the staff weigh heavily on him? On the contrary, Müller seemed to show no stress, but only confidence from the way God so faithfully provided each time a need arose. On 15 July 1839 he wrote: 'How to obtain the means for a dinner, and for what else was needed, I knew not. My heart was perfectly at peace, and unusually sure of help, though I knew not in the least whence it was to come.' Müller added this note for readers of his *Narrative* after another entry recording God's provision in need: 'Dear reader, if you have not the like experience of the Lord's watchful care, Oh taste and see that the Lord is good!'

The prayer times with Müller and the staff at the orphan homes became precious occasions of conversation and petition to their Heavenly Father regarding all the needs of the staff and children, and just as frequently a time of praise and thanksgiving for the answers. For each petition, Müller watched and waited for the answering circumstances, delighting to give God credit for his goodness, and often thanking him even before the answer arrived. And God was as quick to respond, many times answering prayer at the orphan homes while the supplicants were still on their knees.

On a surprising number of other occasions, Müller would unexpectedly meet someone in the street and (without asking, of course) would be handed money for the orphans or the Institution. People continued to donate all manner of household items and clothing, which, if not useful to the homes, were sold for cash (a warehouse in town, shared by the Institution, was used to house and sell the items. We are left to wonder if buyers were found for the elephant teeth and the general's full dress tunic).

Money was regularly put into special collection boxes at the Müller home, at the chapel, and at the orphan houses, and though sometimes it was only a few shillings or pence, the coins might be just enough to help make payment to the milkman or baker. Frequent anonymous gifts were retrieved from the boxes, a number of them with the same handwritten note attached: 'Ecclesiastes 9:10: Whatsoever thy hand findeth to do, do it with thy might...' The postman brought packages filled with items for the work, and often money was tucked in as well.

More than once, a new orphan was sent with the little bit of cash a child was left from his parents' estate, or a donation from the caretaker to help defray expenses (though this was not at all required). No matter that the new resident would increase costs — God would take care of those needs in their time. One desperate day, potatoes from the children's little garden and apples from the tree in the play-yard (used to make apple dumplings) made the most part of a meal for the boys and girls who never suspected the impromptu nature of the menu.

The orphans' own efforts in those early years would sometimes play a small part in keeping the homes afloat. All the girls were taught needlework as part of their curriculum, and their finished projects periodically brought a few critical shillings into the coffers. Both boys and girls were instructed in the art of knitting stockings, a skill that was useful in keeping expenses down at the homes since those clothing items were the ones that most often needed replacing. (The art of darning holes in stockings was just as useful, and universally taught.) A number of times during those lean years, a few pairs of knitted stockings were sold to save the day.

A group of visitors came to visit the boys' orphan home one afternoon. One of the visiting women remarked to the matron: 'Of course, you cannot carry on these institutions without a good stock of funds.' Turning to the matron, a gentleman in the company inquired: 'Have you a good stock?' The matron replied: 'Our funds are deposited in a bank which cannot break.' Tears came to the eyes of the woman; and the gentleman, upon leaving, gave the matron five pounds, urgently needed that day.

'Lord, pity us, even as a father pities his children,' George prayed in April 1842. 'You know we desperately need some oatmeal, some new pairs of shoes, money for the repair of old shoes, and to replenish our stores, and some money for new clothes for the children as well as a little money which is needed for some of the lady helpers. Please send us some large sums.' That same day a letter arrived from the East Indies containing one hundred pounds. Then, as always,

God had answered Müller's prayers and the large amounts had come in exactly when they were most needed. 'I was not the least surprised or excited when this donation came, for I took it as that which came in answer to prayer, and had been long looked for,' Müller explained. No child ever missed a meal, went without shoes, medical care, clothing, caring oversight or education.

In March 1843, for the first time in five years, Müller had a substantial amount of extra money in hand — 300 pounds from a large donation. He had a project in mind for that sum, but told no one until he had prayed for a season. After three weeks he was sure the Lord's hand was in his decision. Another orphan house would be opened, an additional one for older girls. Number 4 Wilson Street had been offered by a family, two very suitable women had expressed interest in being helpers, and fifteen girls who were over the age of seven were ready to move on to the girls' home. He realized that the added home would increase the expenses by several hundred pounds annually, and that years of hard times had recently passed, but he had reason to be confident in his decision. 'I am not tired of this precious way of depending upon the Lord from day to day,' he wrote; 'and thus the faith of other children of God might be strengthened.'

A report on the orphan work was overdue, the last one having been put out two years before. But the update for the year 1844 was the first one not signed by both George Müller and Henry Craik. This was not because of any withdrawal of support or approval by Craik — the two were still working together in perfect harmony, their congregations now consolidated at the Bethany Chapel, after having given up the Gideon Chapel. Mr Craik, though, a paragon of honesty and humility, felt it not right to affix his name to a work carried on almost exclusively by Müller (Craik was to twice refuse an honorary doctorate from St Andrews University). The Scriptural Knowledge Institution and orphan work were now recognized as George Müller's particular ministries. According to his current report, the Institution had sent financial aid to missionaries in Demerara, Upper East Canada, India, Mauritius and Switzerland. In the previous two years, thirty-nine new orphans had been received, totalling 121 in the four homes on Wilson Street. The total income from 10 May 1842 to 14 July 1844 was 24,891 pounds, and one farthing, but God had only begun to show the magnitude of his riches.

8

Larger fields at Ashley Down

The letter delivered to the Müller residence at 21 Paul Street one October morning in 1845 took the recipients unawares. It carried the return address of Wilson Street, and was read with surprised curiosity. 'It's from our neighbours next to the orphan houses,' said Müller. The letter was polite and friendly, but was written to make a point; the four homes in the residential neighbourhood were causing problems for the other families living in the street. The sewage system was hardly adequate for the number of people it serviced; sometimes the water supply couldn't keep up with the demand; and with the children in all four homes using the same small play-yard, it was noisy most of the day. Müller was sensitive to the issues raised, and wanted to do the right thing for everyone, yet he was painfully aware that the waiting list for new orphans just kept growing.

He began to think about the future of the orphan homes in a new light — perhaps it was time to plan for a purpose-built home for the children. He proceeded with his customary method of making decisions: he began praying, asked opinions of respected Christian friends, and made a list of the pros and cons. The complaints of the neighbours he acknowledged as legitimate: there was a problem with the sewage and water, and there was a noticeable din from the busy play-yard. For lack of room on Wilson Street, the children periodically had to be taken to the fields outside of town to give them a chance to run and exercise. Space for a garden would be of great benefit, not only for helping to supply produce for the table, but it could provide a place for the boys to work outdoors. On Wilson Street, the laundry for all four homes had to be sent out because there was not enough space to process it. This was an extra expense and deprived the older girls of training in a necessary household skill. Many of the children arrived in poor health, and the fresh air outside the city limits would be more 'bracing' for them. There was no garden or quiet area for the staff to relax in during 'down' time, and when illness struck at the homes at Wilson Street, there wasn't enough room to give special care to those who were recovering. There just wasn't sufficient room in general.

On the negative side, a large home built especially for the orphans would cost money that Müller didn't have. However, lack of funds had never stopped him from considering a work he determined God wanted him to do. This was one of the conditions Müller taught for praying aright: that one should ask in accordance with God's will, proper motive being the first priority. Also, stressed Müller, prayer should be made in the name of Jesus, to be answered because of his merits and work for us, and not for our own deserving. However, if we continue in known sin, God will not listen to our petitions,

Müller would warn. Finally, one must believe that God is able and willing to answer the prayer. Wait patiently on God, he taught, and continue praying until the answer is received. God sometimes has his reasons to delay until the time is best, but keep watching and waiting, and expect an answer, he urged.

And so George Müller went on praying. He and Mary petitioned God every morning to show them his will in the matter of the purpose-built home. When they were given peace about going ahead, they began to pray for funds to buy a piece of property. In December a gift of one thousand pounds was donated for the orphan work, the largest amount Müller had ever received. 'When I received it,' he remembered, 'I was as calm, as quiet as if I had only received one shilling. For my heart was looking out for answers to my prayers.' Mary's sister came back to Bristol after a visit to London and gave them the news that a Christian architect who had recently read Müller's *Narrative* was interested in his work, and volunteered to design and supervise the construction of the new home.

Müller began to look for a suitable building site and in early February donned his hat, scarf and overcoat to inspect a piece of property on Ashley Down, which from all accounts seemed to be workable and affordable. The property was just north of the city of Bristol, with fresh air and room to grow, but not too far a walk from Bethesda Chapel or the centre of Bristol. He strolled through the acreage, set on the crown of a hill, affording long vistas north and east, and decided it was the best land he had seen so far. The next day he went looking for the landowner, and finding him neither at home nor work, decided to let the matter rest with God for another day. In the morning he was able to speak with the owner, who had already been informed that George Müller was interested in his land. For several hours the night before, the man was unable to sleep, preoccupied with the sale of the property, and had determined that if Müller asked for the land, he would sell the seven acres at 120 pounds per acre, instead of the previously asked-for price of 200 pounds. 'How good is the Lord,' Müller wrote afterwards. '...Observe the hand of God in my not finding the owner at home last evening. The Lord meant to speak to his servant first about this matter.' The agreement was made, and thereafter the hills and meadows of Ashley Down would be known as the location of the new orphan house.

The staff at the four orphan homes also prayed at their regular Saturday night gatherings for God to provide the means for the new construction, and gifts came in. Most of them were small, but four very large ones arrived, adding several thousand pounds to the building fund, with the cost projected to be about 15,000 pounds. In the warm days of August 1847 the cornerstone was laid for the new building, sufficient funds now in hand to begin constructing a home large enough for three hundred children. The 120 orphans on Wilson Street were not neglected during the period of saving for the building fund, all needs being provided as ever. That winter, a gift of one hundred pounds was donated, allowing Müller to buy much-needed suits for all the boys.

Mention must be made at this time of an unhappy episode in the life of Bethesda Chapel. Trouble originated from outside the assembly, yet the fallout profoundly affected the leadership and the flock of believers in Bristol, and altered the direction of the loose fellowship of churches with like beliefs, commonly called the Plymouth Brethren. The fellowship was given that name after a large church in Plymouth where, for a while, a Mr Benjamin Wills Newton was influential. Disagreements and tensions between Mr Newton and John Nelson Darby, a charismatic and capable preacher in Dublin, had developed. In 1847 a more heated animosity erupted over views regarding the nature of the humanity of Christ mentioned in a tract Newton had published.

Müller and Craik regularly had fellowship with both of the men, but disagreed with Newton's statements about Christ's Adamic inheritance through the line of Mary, allowing that he had not sufficiently thought through all the implications of his views. Newton himself, later that year, realized his mistake and published a retraction, but Mr Darby was not satisfied that the error had been disavowed, and continued to denounce Newton. The ensuing tempest in the Plymouth congregation all but destroyed it, and Newton ceased to have any further connection with the Plymouth Brethren movement.

Two members of the Plymouth assembly applied for communion at Bethesda, stirring up controversy among some in the congregation there. It was easily determined that there was no heresy on the part of the two prospective communicants, but when word got out that Bethesda had received supposed followers of Benjamin Newton, Mr Darby decreed that he could never again go to the chapel in Bristol. Later he instructed that all Brethren assemblies should 'judge the Bethesda question'.

Sadly, by 1848 there came to be a division in the assemblies between those who declined to renounce Bethesda (the 'Open Brethren') and those who sided with Darby (the 'Exclusive Brethren'). The Open Brethren held to the belief that each local assembly should maintain its independence and the right to decide who should be received into their fellowship. It was a time of upheaval in the whole movement, the Bethesda Chapel not escaping turmoil with some members leaving, and for a while, divisions pulling apart friends and families. In the maelstrom of accusations, it was intimated that Müller's work among the orphans would come to nothing, but the world would soon see otherwise.

On 18 June 1849, at Ashley Down, three hundred tall windows gleamed in the sunshine, set in a three-storey building of stone. After almost two years of construction, it was the long-expected moving day for the orphans living on Wilson Street. Four days later, following large-scale hauling and organizing, all the children and staff were comfortably settled in, and enthusiasm for the new quarters continued to run high. The orphans were almost as excited about the unaccustomed view out of the windows as they were about their new rooms: cows and green grass instead of street and rooftops. When asked what name the recently opened building would go by, Müller indicated that it should be called 'The New Orphan House, Ashley Down'. He would never allow his own name to be used with the title of the home, frequently pointing out that it was God's orphan home, not Müller's. Every week, five to eight new children arrived from all parts of Great Britain who, when they lost their parents, had nowhere else to go.

In no time the building was full, and the number of the orphans from Wilson Street had more than doubled in a matter of a few months. Yet there were more on the waiting list, and Müller continued to hear about large numbers of children being kept in workhouses, or, even worse, in prisons. Contemplating his ever-growing mission to orphaned children he declared: 'I have served Satan much in my younger years, and I desire now with all my might to serve God during the remaining days of my earthly pilgrimage. I am forty-five and three months old. Every day decreases the number of days that I have to stay on earth. I therefore desire with all my might to work. There are vast multitudes of orphans to be provided for.'

In January 1851, an astoundingly large gift of three thousand pounds was donated for the orphans. Müller began praying about expansion. At the end of May, he announced publicly the plan to build a second home, this time not one for three hundred children, but for seven hundred! Meetings were held in July to advise interested parties of the progress and plans of the orphan houses and other work of the Institution. Henry Craik recorded that the operation headed by his friend and co-pastor nearly made his head spin: 'I felt like a man overpowered by the view of the largeness of the work.'

When Müller announced plans for expansion, the children themselves were among the first to contribute, with their little pences and half-pennies. 'These ... small donations are very sweet to me,' he recorded in his journal. He estimated the cost for the new larger building would be thirty-five thousand pounds. 'The greatness of the sum required,'

Müller wrote, 'affords me a kind of secret joy; for the greater the difficulty to be overcome, the more it will be seen to the glory of God, how much can be done by prayer and faith.' Over the next years gifts arrived for the project, this time a number of them from other countries. Donations came from an Australian shepherd, a young girl from New Zealand who gifted all the egg money from one of her hens, from the United States, China, the East and West Indies, Nova Scotia, Tahiti, Canada, India, Ceylon, Africa, Turkey, France, Switzerland, Germany and Italy. People around the world were reading about the New Orphan Home in Müller's *Narrative* or in the yearly reports from Ashley Down, and wanted to do their bit to help.

Müller's orphan work was building momentum, but a sad interval punctuated the life of the family. Dr Anthony Groves, Mary's brother, who had been doing mission work in Chittoor, India, had come back to England in the autumn of 1852 because of ill health, his young family remaining behind to continue the work. He visited Bristol to see his sister and brother-in-law, and was impressed with their work at the New Orphan House: 'the untiring devotion to it of dear George and Mary, and Lydia,' he wrote in his memoir, 'walking there and back every day, and working there all day long. They seem so to love the children.' For a while he appeared to be feeling better, doing a little speaking and travelling, but in the spring he took a turn for the worse, and doctors diagnosed him with terminal stomach cancer. His family set out to join him, leaving India as soon as Dr Groves had notified them. When he knew the end was near, he came to stay with the Müllers, the only home he had in England, ministered to lovingly by George, Mary, Lydia, and two of his other sisters. He fell asleep in Jesus 20 May 1853, his wife and children not arriving from India until three months later.

As Müller collected funds for the second building, the number of names on the New Orphan House waiting list continued to climb — reaching the hundreds. He began praying for large donations to come in so that the construction could begin as soon as possible. God answered that prayer with five big donations, so that in 1857, six years after the project was conceived, a new building was completed and furnished. The plans had changed, however, and the second building was designed to hold only 400 children, constructed on the original piece of property at right angles to the first house. Another separate building would be built to house the other 300 children projected to be cared for at Ashley Down, and Müller kept praying for funds. In 1858, he was able to purchase eleven and a half acres across the street from the other two houses, and with room enough to build a home larger than anticipated, the house was planned to hold 450 children. Completed in 1862, house number three was the largest and most prominent of the buildings, and where Müller was from then on to have his office. It brought the total capacity at Ashley Down to 1,150 children.

As Müller had waited for funds to come in for buildings two and three, he was praying all along that God would choose and prepare the hearts of the helpers who would be best qualified to work with the children. When opening day came, each house immediately needed its own staff, a dedicated group of Christian adults who would be instructors, nurses, masters and matrons, all doing their best with God's help to be surrogate parents. Each home was run independently, the several wings having at least two different schools in each, and an infirmary on the top floor. The children would meet together in the buildings' large dining rooms for meal-times and chapel services.

By the time House Number Three opened, the Müllers had been taking care of the physical needs of orphans for twenty-six years and knew how to do it efficiently, with precise organization and a well-followed schedule critical in an institution the size of the operation at Ashley Down. The children rose at six o'clock, and by seven were at work with pre-breakfast duties. The morning meal was at eight, followed by a half-hour devotional service, and school beginning at 10.00. After the 1.00 lunch, school resumed until about 4.30, when an hour and a half of outdoor exercise began. The last meal was at 6.00. Food in the dining halls of Ashley Down was nutritious, and likely far better than what most of the children were previously used to, but by today's standards might be considered monotonous — oatmeal was eaten every morning, shipped from Scotland by the ton.

Personal items for the children were uniformly and efficiently managed. Each child had a small numbered bag in the bathing room for his own comb and hair brush. All the older boys wore a navy blue jacket, cut short to the waist, white collars, brown corduroy trousers and caps. They each had three suits of clothing and a cloak to wear in bad weather. The younger boys wore blue shorts and white smocks for every day. Washable clothing had the child's own number on each piece, with another number indicating the rotation in which the clothing would be worn.

Each girl had five dresses. For every day, the girls wore a navy blue dress with small white dots, and for church-wear in warm weather, a lavender cotton dress with a small matching cape. The girls wore white cotton stockings in summer and black wool in winter. When they went out, they tied on their bonnets of straw trimmed with a green and white checked ribbon. (These uniforms, which were fashionable for children in the 1850s, were worn without any substantial change in style until 1936, taking on a quaint look for several decades.)

On any given Sunday between ten and eleven o'clock in the morning, hundreds of identically-dressed children, the boys with their dark caps bobbling as they stepped, and the girls in a flurry of lavender, could be seen trudging in neat rows up the hills of Bristol. They were on their way home to Ashley Down after attending church at the Bethesda Chapel, walking sermons on a prayer-answering God.

During the week, the girls who were over fourteen and who had finished their classroom work could be distinguished by their white aprons tied in the back with strings. They were the 'House Girls'. The oldest girls, nearing readiness to be sent out to a position, were 'Cap Girls', identified by their white caps, aprons to the waist, and white collars. The homes couldn't have functioned without the help of the House Girls and Cap Girls in the kitchens, dining rooms, laundry, parlours, nurseries and at the sewing machines. For their work, they were given a salary of six shillings a week, three of them to be banked until they left the orphan home to start their first job.

Müller was criticized by some for over-educating the children in his New Orphan Home — those who felt that poor children should not be given skills and expectations beyond their position in society. A few even dared to accuse him of depriving the community of unskilled labourers. But Müller saw each child as important in God's eyes and put such a high stock in education that he hired an inspector for the several schools at Ashley Down and the day schools in town run by the Scriptural Knowledge Institution. Every year in February and March the boys and girls were tested to make sure they were competent in their studies, according to government standards. In the year 1885 it was recorded that the average percentage on the exams was 91.1. The curriculum consisted of reading, writing, arithmetic, dictation, grammar, geography, history, composition, singing, Swedish exercise, needlework and, of course, Bible. Daily, the children were assigned a Scripture verse to learn, and on Sunday were required to recite the verses from the six previous days. In the classroom, the Bible was taught as the inspired Word of God, and Scripture quotations or inspirational messages written with cut-out letters often decorated the walls of the dining hall and schools at the New Home.

Besides knitting, the girls' instruction included sewing samplers, making their own dresses and mending; the boys were required to knit three pairs of socks for themselves before they left the homes. One 'old orphan', a Mr W. Tidball, revealed to Müller's biographer, Nancy Garton, that the hand-knit socks became an object of barter at times. On George Müller's birthday, 27 September, the one day of the year the children were served a special apple dumpling dessert, a pair of socks might get a boy an extra dumpling in trade from one who was behind in his knitting.

The girls usually stayed at the home until they were at least seventeen, when a position was found for them, almost always involving domestic work in a household. A few were trained as nurses. At the age of fourteen or fifteen, boys were sent to learn an occupation, usually being apprenticed to a tradesman, craftsman or clerk of some kind, the apprenticeship normally costing the orphan home the approximate amount of support for one year. Pains were taken to find Christian homes and employers for all the graduating orphans. For that reason, advertisement was never made for apprentice positions, Müller hoping to avoid situations where a boy might be taken on only for the stipend. As the years went by, a plan to train well-suited young men and women to be teachers was developed, and from that programme came many a fine instructor for the day schools supported by the Scriptural Knowledge Institution, and for the orphan homes themselves.

Living at the orphan home wasn't all lessons and work; there were special holidays and fun times. Every summer there was a day-long outing to the meadows of Purdown, a mile and a half away. The children were given cloth bags of sweet treats to snack on while they hiked to the meadow in a long trailing line, their picnic blankets in arm. They played games in the grass and under the trees, and were fed lunch and tea from hampers delivered by the staff — a time once a year when the boys and girls from all the houses could mingle with each other. The day ended with the launching of fire balloons, one for each house, in the dusk of the long holiday

(fire balloons were a miniature version of hot-air balloons
— now recognized to be a hazard, and illegal in most areas).

Christmas was a time of great activity and excitement with
plays, parties, singing, and holiday decorations throughout
the homes. The children were always allowed to express
creativity by decorating their rooms, but Christmas afforded
even more opportunity for embellishment. Each house had
its own big decorated tree, which became loaded with gifts
by the time the holiday arrived — at that season, donations
of toys and special foods came in abundance. One notable
year, 150 pheasants were sent by a donor in Cornwall.
Christmas sweet shops were opened for the children in
each house, where they could purchase goodies from an
appealing selection with their small holiday allowances. The
children considered it a special treat to have Mr and Mrs
Müller join them in their festivities.

George Müller was usually a very even-tempered man, but
was sorely tried at the occasional rumour that his orphans
were not treated well or were in some way deprived. Charles
Dickens one day came to visit the New Orphan Home in
Bristol, presumably to investigate a negative story he had
heard about the care of the children at Ashley Down. Müller
didn't write of this visit in his *Narrative*, but it was recorded
in Dickens' own weekly journal, *Household Words*. Müller
received him courteously and, assessing the situation,
decided to let Dickens see for himself the conditions at the
New Orphan Home. He handed a large collection of keys to
an aide and instructed him to show Mr Dickens any part of
the homes he desired to see — and Dickens recorded that he
went away fully satisfied.

George Müller did everything he could to make the orphan houses at Ashley Down a good home for children. The best possible attention was given to their outward condition, but he knew that the inward condition of his orphans could only be made right by God. He himself was an example of one who had been given the best of material things in his youth, yet whose thoughts and heart were far from the Saviour. And so he prayed that each child might embrace the good news of Jesus Christ and his loving atonement. Many hundreds of children made a profession of faith while at the homes, perhaps after a special service, or because a teacher or even a classmate had spoken with them. In some years there were periods when a large number of children at one time came to faith and requested permission to have their own prayer meetings. There was no pressure to make a profession, however, and Müller was not insistent that the graduates worship at Bethesda or its sister churches. Attendance at any church that taught the Bible as the Word of God was encouraged, but it gave Müller special pleasure when children from the orphan home or the Sunday schools requested to join as communicants of the Bethesda assembly. He realized though that God's timing in each life is different and that the evidence of his working may be seen years later: '...we reap already abundantly even now, but the chief part of the harvest is yet awaiting us,' Müller wrote.

9

Abundant harvest

While construction workers at House Number Three laboured in the cold of January 1860, a baby boy was born in London. He was named William. The boy was the tenth child in a family which, because of the father's alcoholism, lived in a London workhouse. By the time William was five, both parents had died and the children were on their own, William ending up on the streets of London, always on the look-out for a warm place to sleep, or a bite to eat. He had learned a few acrobatic tricks and some comic songs to perform that would sometimes earn him a few pence, and occasionally had opportunity to work at the Covent Garden market, hauling great boxes in the pre-dawn chill. There were times, though, that an old cigar or orange peel were the only things he could find to put in his stomach.

Müller had been thinking about boys like William. His first priority had always been the girls, who he felt needed more protection, and up to an older age than the boys, but it troubled him that the waiting list, fast approaching one thousand and growing every week, held so many boys' names. He prayed that God would somehow allow him to build two more houses, a fourth and a fifth, on the land across the street, making room for 850 more orphans. The cost would exceed fifty thousand pounds, and the land wasn't even for sale, but Müller knew God could make anything happen. After all, he owned all the treasures in the world. He added this request to the many he prayed about every morning after his Bible reading.

George and Mary also prayed together after family devotions later in the morning, and reserved the last hour in the late afternoon before they left the orphan home to approach God's throne with one voice. If there were pressing issues, additional times were added to make supplication to the Lord. On the prayer list would be finances, of course, but other matters of great importance: specific difficulties with some of the children, good employers for their graduating orphans, and health for the children and staff (epidemics of scarlet fever, whooping cough, cholera, measles, typhus and smallpox passed through the vicinity during Müller's time, but relatively few children were lost. A one per cent annual death rate at the homes was about the average, and thought to be quite low). Fervent petitions were also made for the salvation of individuals — Müller prayed decades for some — and revival and spiritual growth in the church and among the children.

At one point a boiler was at the top of the prayer list. In late November 1857, there was trouble at House Number One. The boiler feeding the entire heating system, though only eight years old, developed an alarming leak. It was encased in brick, and would possibly need total replacement, a time-consuming job which would shut down the entire heating system until finished. Müller decided to have the bricking removed to identify the problem — which had to be fixed one way or another to get through the winter — and arranged a date for the workmen to start. Before the time came, the first bitter cold north winds of winter began to blow. The boiler would need to be shut down, but how could three hundred children be kept warm during repairs? There was no safe temporary heating solution and certainly no place to move that many children. As the north wind steadily whistled across the meadows, prayer was made: 'Lord, these are *thy* orphans: be pleased to change this north wind into a south wind, and give the workmen a mind to work that the job may be speedily done.'

On the very same day the workmen arrived, the frigid northerly wind was replaced by a warm breeze from the south, and after the demolition was done, the workers informed the foreman that they would prefer to work all night at the repairs instead of returning in the morning. The source of the leak was discovered, and, with no little difficulty, was repaired. Within thirty hours, the fires were re-lit, and until the time the boiler was putting out hot water and heating the air throughout the building, the mild south wind blew, keeping all three hundred children comfortably warm.

Many were curious about the faith-run orphan homes at Ashley Down. Müller's institution had been the first of its type, and people wanted to see what went on there. Each house was open to visitors on a different day of the week, and thousands came for a tour, Müller taking the opportunity to show all how every need had been met through God's provision.

In 1865 a young missionary arrived for a visit, having been inspired by Müller early in his life. Hudson Taylor had already been working in China for six years and with him was a party of just-commissioned missionaries, members of the newly formed China Inland Mission. Taylor had begun the mission along the same principles as the orphan home, and on that visit to Ashley Down was encouraged by Müller in faith and prayer and other practical matters important to foreign workers. He commended to Taylor the reading of the Bible consecutively and in its entirety. 'I will pray for you,' Mr Müller promised as the group left for their work in the Far East.

Though suffering numerous periods of ill health when a young man, Müller seemed to be blessed with a second wind in his mature years, putting in long days to maintain his huge workload with the orphan homes, the Institution and Bethesda Chapel. Arthur T. Pierson, early biographer who was personally acquainted with Müller, described his friend at that point in his life:

> His form was tall and slim, always neatly attired, and very erect, and his step firm and strong. His countenance, in repose, might have been thought stern, but for the smile which so habitually lit up his eyes and played over his features that it left its impress on the lines of his face. His manner was one of simple courtesy and unstudied dignity: no one in his presence have felt like vain trifling, and there

was about him a certain indescribable air of authority and
majesty that reminded one of a born prince; and yet there
was mingled with all this a simplicity as childlike that even
children felt themselves at home with him. In his speech,
he never quite lost that particular foreign quality known
as accent, and he always spoke with slow and measured
articulation, as though a double watch were set at the door
of his lips...

Henry Craik, who was the same age as George, continued to struggle with his health. He wasn't one to complain, but revealed in his journals the many times he had to push through the days fighting exhaustion and discomfort. He had been diagnosed with a heart condition, and by the time he was sixty, it was obvious he was failing. Müller visited his friend frequently with prayer and encouragement, but one day in January 1866, Craik was too weak to speak. He requested that Müller and Mrs Craik sit by his bedside if only to look upon them. It was the last time Müller was to see his beloved yoke-fellow and prayer partner, their friendship of thirty-six years never wavering. Craik's death was a great personal loss to Müller, as well as to the Bethesda Fellowship.

The three full-time personal assistants who were helping Müller starting in the early 1860s were a godsend for the busy director and pastor. They handled much of the heavy correspondence of the homes and the Institution as well as most of the day-to-day paperwork and accounting. Mary was working hard too, helping in any way she could — ordering fabric for clothes, underwear and blankets, checking invoices, making up a clean bed for a child, or visiting those recovering in the infirmary. She made each child feel special with a smile and a pat.

Donations for the construction of the projected buildings four and five came in slowly at first as Müller prayed, and he computed it would take twenty-five years to collect the needed sum at that rate. Then came a shower of large gifts. The eighteen-acre plot of land across the street was bought, with the difficulties worked out just as Müller had expected God would do. Next were the jobs of building, furnishing and equipping the homes. There would be room for nine hundred new orphans when they were done, making two thousand and fifty orphans all together at Ashley Down.

George and Mary laboured harder than ever. Just the correspondence required for admitting the new orphans was staggering. Of considerable help was daughter Lydia, who by then had already worked for many years at the orphan homes without salary. Freely giving of her time and energy also was Mary's sister, Lydia Groves, a fixture at Ashley Down.

Mrs Müller's health had never been good; however, she was not one to pay heed to bodily discomfort — so George saw to it that she rested half an hour after the noon meal, sitting quietly with her hand in his. Müller fussed with his wife about slowing down and taking care of herself, but she couldn't be convinced to work less, steadfastly overseeing the provision of bedding and clothing for the hundreds of new children to arrive virtually en masse.

In November 1868, the first orphan was welcomed to House Number Four. By that time Mary felt her strength waning, and was thinking her time on earth was near the end; yet she had fond hopes of seeing building number five open: '... but most of all,' she told her husband, 'I wish that the Lord Jesus would come, and that we might all go together.' A little more than a year later, in January 1870, House Number Five was accepting children; but soon after the opening, Mary became sick. After several weeks, on a Monday afternoon, she had worsened so much a doctor was called and she was sent to bed. The doctor diagnosed rheumatic fever, and it was clear to all that Mrs Müller was seriously ill.

She died on Sunday afternoon of the following week, at the age of seventy-two, ending forty years of marriage to her adoring husband. Müller was broken-hearted, but accepted the Lord's will in her home-going, and preached at her funeral sermon from Psalm 119:68: 'Thou art good, and doest good.' He couldn't argue with God's plan, and though he knew his wife was home in glory, he struggled daily with her loss and missed her more and more as time went on. 'The lovely one is no more with me, to share my joys and sorrows,' he said to his congregation.

Lydia faithfully and efficiently took her mother's place at the house that winter and in the orphanage, where wave after wave of children came in to fill House Number Five. Shortly after his wife's death, Müller asked James Wright, a younger man whom he had known for some time, to come and help him at Ashley Down. Mr Wright had worked with Müller on projects of the Scriptural Knowledge Institution and at the Bethesda Chapel and was loved by all for his cheerful smile, his kind ways and his beautiful bass voice. He had agreed to take the reins of the homes at Ashley Down when the time came that Müller was no longer able to continue in that capacity.

Another winter came and went, then spring blossomed, and was followed by the sunny days of August, one of which brought Mr Wright tentatively into the director's office. He came to ask a personal question: 'Will you allow me to ask for your daughter's hand in marriage?' Müller was surprised — his daughter was a thirty-nine-year-old spinster — but was pleased. He gave an affirmative answer to Wright, and wrote of his happiness: 'I knew no one to whom I could so willingly entrust this my choicest earthly treasure.' Lydia, however, seemed to be paralyzed by indecision, and was in a state of inner turmoil for about two weeks. When she confessed that her reticence was due to the thought of leaving her father — whom she knew still keenly missed his wife — he was able to convince her that marriage to such a fine man would be a source of joy and comfort to him.

Not long after that, another surprising proposal occurred. Müller asked a Miss Susannah Grace Sangar to be his wife. Although the decision to wed had been a matter of much personal prayer, the announcement, according to his nephew (Edward, Anthony Groves' son), was a shock to most in his congregation. One might suppose Müller gave them no forewarning in the way of the usual signs of a growing relationship. Susannah was about fifteen years younger than Müller, a governess in Clifton, and a woman whom Müller had known for twenty-five years as a 'consistent Christian, and regarding whom I had every reason to believe that she would prove a helper to me in my various services.' They were married in November 1872, two weeks after James and Lydia.

Susannah was not a woman of means, but gave up all she had and placed her lot in with that of her new husband, who was trusting only in God to provide his needs. Her interests and gifts were not the same as the first Mrs Müller's, and Susannah never did find a place of service working directly with the orphans, but lent her energy to support Mr Müller in the duties that fell upon him.

People from all over the world continued to generously support Müller and the work of the orphan home at Ashley Down. He recorded each gift as he had for so many years, and sent out yearly reports, always giving God the credit for everything that was accomplished. He urged his readers in the same way to 'expect great things from God, and to trust Him at all times, and under all circumstances'.

Some gifts came with a note attached explaining the source of the gift: the money had been saved by not using sugar in cups of tea, not taking a vacation that year, not buying a new bonnet, or some other sacrifice for the sake of the orphans. Müller printed some of the notes and other letters he received at the orphan home in his reports. Many were from men and women who had lived at Ashley Down as children, and who wanted to express their thanks, such as the following note: 'Beloved and respected Sir, I cannot feel grateful enough to you for all the kindness I received whilst under your fatherly care in the dear Orphan House, and the years I spent there I can truly say were the happiest I ever spent in my life...'

Each child admitted to the homes had a different story, but all had the same need for love and care as they grew up in the absence of their parents. However, they weren't always as happy to be at Ashley Down as the writer of the aforementioned letter. Twelve-year-old William arrived from London in 1872, being sent by a Christian man working at a mission in that city. William had come to the man's attention performing acrobatics and tricks in the street, and it was verified the boy was, as suspected, an orphan living on his own. The enterprising lad was that same William who had been born in the poorhouse and had never had a home. He wasn't happy to be shut inside the great stone building at Ashley Down, stripped of his old clothes, and scrubbed and outfitted with a starched collar and stiff pants.

It was discovered the next day that William, like many children who came to the homes, had never been to school and was ignorant of the most basic knowledge — such as the letters of the alphabet. The structured life in the homes was an adjustment for the once-roving boy, and he got into a number of scrapes and mischief, one night leading a raid on the staff dining room. In the end he was won over by kindness, and for the first time learned about the God of the Bible, Jesus Christ, and his sacrifice for fallen man. He became a good student and developed a circle of friends to whom he was glad to teach his acrobatic tricks — for a small fee.

When William was sixteen, a position was found for him as an apprentice to a flour miller, and on his last day at the orphan home he was called in to see Mr Müller for a final visit. He described later in his memoirs what happened in the director's prayer room: Müller placed a Bible in William's right hand, and in his left, a half-crown coin.

'You can hold tighter with your right hand than with your left, can you not?' said Müller.

'Yes, sir,' answered William.

'Well, my lad, hold to the teaching of that book and you will always have something for your left hand to hold,' said Müller, who asked William to kneel, and then prayed for God's blessing on him with hand on head.

His new master was a Christian, and through his kind example, the seeds of the gospel that were planted at the orphan home produced fruit, and William counted himself a believer in Jesus Christ. He eventually became a loved and well-respected minister in New Zealand, later writing about the orphan home: 'I can see now that it was just the place for me and what a blessing it was that I was sent there.'

10

Scattering the seed

'Dear Mr Müller, I do not wish to flatter you,' said the preacher, 'but I consider it my duty to tell you, for your encouragement, that this has been the happiest day of my whole life.' The Müllers spent September and October 1874 on the Isle of Wight, Susannah recovering from a near-fatal bout of typhoid, and while there Müller preached several times for a fellow pastor in one of the nonconformist chapels. His sermon there on the last day occasioned the appreciative comment from the local preacher.

When the Müllers returned to Bristol — Susannah much recovered — he pondered the preacher's surprising remark, and the encouragement he and the congregation on the Isle of Wight had received. His thoughts revisited the long-lived desire to do the work of a missionary, and the thoughts were followed by prayer. By that time, there were several capable leaders and teachers at the Bethesda Fellowship, and James and Lydia were efficiently running the orphan homes, so that Müller could absent himself without causing the work to suffer. His new wife loved to travel, a good companion for him, who in his seventieth year was contemplating a new phase of ministry — addressing audiences outside of Bristol.

As one would expect from Müller, he carefully prayed and deliberated over his motives to do travelling missionary work, setting down in writing the matters he felt needful to address: he would preach the simple gospel, encourage believers in their security and privileges in Christ, point believers back to the Bible, promote among Christians a spirit of brotherly love instead of divisiveness, strengthen believers' trust in God by his own examples of answered prayer, promote separation from the culture of the world, and fix the hope of Christians on the return of Christ.

On 26 March 1875 Müller and wife Susannah embarked on the first in a series of missionary journeys which would last a total of seventeen years. Their trips took them to forty-two countries, and according to Müller (who, as we know, kept excellent statistics), involved two hundred thousand miles of travel by land and sea. An account of the trips up to the eleventh journey may be found in his *Narratives* and are also described in whole by Mrs Müller in her book, *The Preaching Tours and Missionary Labours of George Müller*. Both accounts impress the reader with the length and difficulty of some of the trips (one was two years and seven months), the number of times Müller spoke, and the frequent large crowds of people who came to hear him — Müller estimating he spoke to at least three million people on his travels.

Five of the tours took place in Great Britain. On the first trip he spoke seventy times, one of his engagements being at the well-filled Metropolitan Tabernacle in London where Charles Spurgeon ministered. The two preachers held each other in mutual respect, enjoying a friendship over many years. Their preaching styles, however, were completely different. Müller was not known for the type of oratory that Spurgeon used, but was considered to be more of a teacher, sweet earnestness persuading his listeners. Spurgeon remarked after one of his messages: 'The diction and structure of the discourse were not above the average Sunday school teacher, but *there was the man behind it*.'

Müller's second tour was for the express purpose of following up the evangelistic crusade of Dwight Moody and Ira Sankey, who had just returned to America after an extremely successful campaign in Great Britain. Müller drew thousands of believers in Jesus and seekers alike in England, Scotland and Ireland, giving them encouragement in the faith. 'The living God is living still,' he proclaimed with confidence.

All around Great Britain, Müller came across 'old boys' and 'old girls' from the orphan homes, who came to see their beloved benefactor. In Liverpool, a weather-beaten captain of a merchant vessel, who as a boy lived at Ashley Down, came to hear him. When he first walked through the door, he was still unconverted, but after hearing the gospel from the grey-haired Müller, the same he heard before as a child, he wept in final apprehension of God's great gift for him.

Three times the Müllers travelled to Canada and the United States. In 1877, on the first trip when bound for Quebec, their ship the *Sardinian* was making good time until it ran into dense fog off Newfoundland. Müller realized that the drastic reduction in speed could delay their docking, and informed Captain Dutton that he had to be in Quebec by that Saturday afternoon.

'It is impossible,' said the captain.

Müller requested the two of them go down to the chart room to pray about the situation, Captain Dutton reluctantly indulging him. Müller knelt down and made simple petition, and when the captain began to take his turn praying, Müller put his hand on his shoulder.

'Do not pray. First, you don't believe He will answer, and second, I believe He has and there is no need whatever for you to pray about it. Captain, I have known my Lord for fifty-two years, and there has never been a single day that I have failed to get an audience with the King.'

As Captain Dutton related many times later, the fog was already lifting when they emerged on deck, and the Müllers made their engagement in ample time.

From Niagara Falls, the couple entered the United States and began their tour there, Müller speaking coast to coast in churches, schools and institutions, to audiences both white and African-American. In the U.S. he also encountered a few of his old orphans who had emigrated, and who were delighted to have an unexpected chance to see the good Mr Müller again. One of the highlights of the tour was an opportunity to speak in the church founded by George Whitefield, the man whose biography had inspired him so many years before to prayerfully read the Scriptures on his knees. The Old Presbyterian Church in Newburyport owned a Bible used by Whitefield, and granted rare permission to let Mr Müller use it in preaching. Also on that journey, the travellers were invited by President Hayes and his wife for a special visit to the White House, Müller and the President chatting for about half an hour and Mrs Hayes leading a tour of the presidential home.

Journeys to the European continent were made five separate times, where the evangelist was able to use his French and German language skills. Müller was glad to show his wife the University of Halle, and the great Francke Orphanage, whose founder had so inspired him in his own orphan work. He spoke twice in the large hall there, and was delighted to once again find his old professor and friend, Dr Tholuck, still living in Halle. When in Holland, he made visit to an orphanage, this one begun after the founder had read about Müller's efforts at Ashley Down. He also was depending only on God to supply the needs of the 450 children living there. In Barcelona and Madrid, the Müllers had the privilege of visiting schools the Scriptural Knowledge Institution had been supporting for ten years. Müller spoke to the children through a Spanish interpreter, telling them that he was praying they might all meet again some day in heaven, forgiven because of the blood of the Lord Jesus.

The year 1882 brought Mr Müller and his wife to his birthplace in Kroppenstaedt, Germany. George had not seen the little town for sixty-four years and felt privileged to bear witness to his Lord twice in the largest meeting hall there. That same year, he experienced first-hand in Russia how Christians were being more and more restricted in their witness and worship together.

Their trip to the Near East in 1881–1882 was one of the most difficult in terms of travel comforts. Mr and Mrs Müller visited Egypt, Palestine, Syria, Asia Minor, Turkey and Greece, riding in open wagons on bad roads, and sometimes astride donkeys. In Jaffa they experienced a hair-raising transport to their steamship in heavy seas via a boat rowed by eight Arabs.

Twice the Müllers made the long trip to Australia, travelling there in 1885 and 1887. On the first trip, they continued on to Java, Hong Kong and then to China where they visited with Hudson Taylor and members of the China Inland Mission team. Müller was able to see first-hand some of the work that had long been supported by the Institution. On their second visit to Australia, they travelled further to Tasmania and New Zealand, then sailed north to India for their second visit there. Beginning in September 1883, the Müllers had spent eight months in India, Müller finally able to realize his desire to do missionary work in the 'East Indies'. He spoke 206 times and travelled 21,000 miles on that first trip.

During the second Indian journey, Müller preached a number of times in Calcutta, where the temperatures soared. On a train leaving the city for cooler climes, he became very ill, and Susannah used every resource she could to keep him hydrated and cool. She was afraid he was dying, but God showed him mercy, and he revived as they travelled to the more temperate foothills of the Himalayas. Müller was eighty-three, and had come to greatly appreciate the capable help of his wife, recognizing that his beloved Mary would never have been able to travel with him the way Susannah did.

James Wright kept in close touch with Müller while he was journeying, the two endeavouring to communicate regarding the needs and plans of the work in Bristol on a weekly basis. However, while the Müllers were in Jubbulpore in 1890, they received an unexpected communication from Bristol. An urgent telegram was sent from Mr Wright, informing of the sudden death of his wife, and Müller's only child, Lydia. Müller described the news as a 'heavy blow', but was comforted by the knowledge that nothing is outside of God's plan. The couple secured travel home as soon as possible to comfort and help the bereaved James Wright.

Müller and his wife continued to travel until he was eighty-seven years old, when they settled into a more tame routine within the confines of Bristol. George assisted James every day at the orphan home, worked on projects of the Scriptural Knowledge Institution and preached at Bethesda Chapel or one of its sister churches. (There were 1,200 people among the four congregations in the Bristol area that operated as one, all begun by the Bethesda congregation, and six additional church plants running independently.) The Institution was now providing Bibles in at least twelve languages, and still supporting dozens of missionaries and many Sunday schools around the world. Since it had begun in 1834, it had not only circulated over a million and a half Bibles and portions of Scripture, but over *one hundred million* other Christian books, pamphlets and tracts.

Susannah, although younger than George and an energetic companion on their many long trips, suddenly became ill in 1894. They had been married for twenty-three years, but no more were to follow. When his wife passed away, Müller found himself living alone on Paul Street and decided to give up his home, moving into House Number Three at Ashley Down. His health was still good, and he could often be seen walking in his long strides around the orphan home, busy at work.

When George was ninety-one, the country commemorated Queen Victoria's Diamond Jubilee in June. Müller arranged for the children at Ashley Down to celebrate her sixty-year reign with a trip to nearby Clifton Zoo, financed by a special donation from the city of Bristol. Müller remembered that long-ago day when the young queen was crowned and recalled that his first orphan home was already in operation, having opened the year before. On the eve of Jubilee Sunday he preached at Bethesda Chapel, as he had done many hundreds of times before. Standing as tall and straight as ever and with a strong clear voice, he spoke from Psalm 23, finishing with a description of the precious blessedness of the Christian who lives in the presence of God. 'Surely goodness and mercy shall follow me all the days of my life...'

The next winter, after his ninety-second birthday, he preached a memorable message one weekday evening to a large crowd at the Market Street Chapel. 'I am a happy old man,' he said with energy and a smile on his face, 'yes, indeed, I am a happy old man! I walk about my room, and I say, "Lord Jesus, I am not alone, for You are with me. I have buried my wives and my children, but You are left. I am never lonely or desolate with You and with Your smile, which is better than life itself!!'"

One of the lessons Müller was recorded to have preached on his missionary journeys was that 'the chief business of every day is first of all to seek to be truly at rest and happy in God'. Müller found his happiness every morning reading Scripture and praying over those holy words. It was said that he had read through the Bible nearly two hundred times, the last hundred on his knees, never tiring of rising early to meet with his Lord. On the morning of 10 March 1898, Müller didn't get a chance to open his Bible, but met the Lord Jesus face to face early that day. He was found on the floor next to his bed at 7 o'clock, when a cup of tea was taken to his room.

Some would say Mr Müller was a poor man when he died — all he possessed were a few pounds in the bank and some very plain furniture. But his treasures were laid up elsewhere. Four days after Müller's death, James Wright spoke to the assembled children at 9.00 on the morning of the funeral, but was hardly able to proceed because of their loud grieving. There was great mourning also in many corners of the world, far from Bristol. When the funeral procession left Orphan House Number Three, the bier was followed not by any blood relatives of George Müller, but by some of his children — there were over ten thousand to that date. Walking in the procession were four individuals who had been residents at the first orphan home on Wilson Street. Along with them were children currently living at Ashley Down, many faces unashamedly wet with tears. The citizens of Bristol lined the streets in homage — tens of thousands of them.

Bethesda Chapel was not able to contain all who came for the service that Monday, where James Wright and others called to remembrance the life that was George Müller's. Mr Wright read from Hebrews 13:7-8: 'Remember them which have the rule over you, who have spoken the word of God, whose faith follow, considering the end of their conversation: Jesus Christ the same yesterday, and today, and for ever.' He urged his listeners to imitate the faith which Müller had modelled and preached, reminding them of what he had often said: 'Never let enter your minds a shadow of doubt as to the love of the Father's heart or the power of the Father's arm.'

A conversation Müller had recently had with a friend was related by another speaker — illustrating his dependence on the Lord. 'When God calls you home, it will be like a ship going into harbour, full sail,' his friend had remarked. 'Oh no!' replied Mr Müller, 'It is poor George Müller who needs daily to pray, "Hold Thou me up in my goings, that my footsteps slip not."'

After the service, some eighty carriages joined the funeral procession as it travelled to Arnos Vale cemetery across the river from the centre of Bristol. At his own request, there were no flowers or ostentation — under a tree next to the graves of Mary and Susannah, George Müller was laid to rest in a plain elm coffin. In the succeeding days, a number of the orphans, some grown and some still at the homes, sent donations for a marker, and James Wright, in order to honour his friend's wishes for only a modest headstone, had to ask that no more be given. His enduring memory would live on in the lives of the thousands he blessed, and in his example of faith and trust in God.

The legacy of George Müller

'But without faith it is impossible to please him,' the Bible declares in Hebrews 11:6, 'for he that cometh to God must believe that he is, and that he is a rewarder of them that diligently seek him.' This was the lived-out testimony of George Müller, who claimed that God had rewarded him with at least fifty thousand answers to prayer. Some have said Müller's faith in God's hearing and answering prayer was childlike. He would have taken no offence. His childlike faith was rewarded with the blessing of being used by God to bring thousands of individuals to faith in Jesus Christ, through his preaching in Bristol, the orphan homes, the distribution of Scripture by the Scriptural Knowledge Institution, aid to missionaries, and his worldwide evangelism campaign.

Though Müller never had the intention of beginning a new movement, the Open Brethren own Müller and Craik as among the founding fathers of their fellowship. Both also made great contribution to the development of the faith missions movement — workers sent out without any specific denominational support. Not only did the Institution support missionaries serving around the world, but sixty-three members from the Bethesda assembly followed God's calling to foreign fields.

After sixty-two years under the direction of George Müller, the orphan work continued with a series of godly administrators, beginning with James Wright. All continued Müller's practice of depending on God, through prayer, for the needs of the orphans. They were well provided for, even during the difficult times of two world wars, the homes at Ashley Down giving children the same kind of excellent care, teaching and Christian shepherding as they received when Müller was at the helm. In 1948, the trustees decided to sell the large homes at Ashley Down to buy smaller residences for family group homes which could better meet the needs of parentless children in that generation. The George Müller Charitable Trust, working under the name 'Müllers', still operates Christian ministries helping children and families.

The Scriptural Knowledge Institution for Home and Abroad exists today as part of the George Müller Charitable Trust and sends monthly financial help to mission works at home and overseas. It aids orphans around the globe in numbers even more plentiful than the total residents at Ashley Down in Müller's time. The institution also runs a Christian home for the elderly.

Müller, who originally had doubts and some trepidation at the printing of his autobiography, was later convinced of the impact it was having on his generation. *A Narrative of Some of the Lord's Dealings with George Müller* circulated not only in the United Kingdom, but worldwide. Portions of Müller's autobiography are still in print, still blessing readers with the challenge of faith in Jesus Christ and believing prayer.